Clark Baldwin, The Serial Killing Trucker

Ruth Kanton

Published by Trellis Publishing, 2021.

While every precaution has been taken in the preparation of this book, the publisher assumes no responsibility for errors or omissions, or for damages resulting from the use of the information contained herein.

CLARK BALDWIN, THE SERIAL KILLING TRUCKER

First edition. July 10, 2021.

Copyright © 2021 Ruth Kanton.

ISBN: 979-8224367962

Written by Ruth Kanton.

CLARK BALDWIN, THE SERIAL KILLING TRUCKER

RUTH KANTON

Clark Perry Baldwin

On Wednesday May 6, 2020, investigators arrived at Clark Perry Baldwin's home in Waterloo, Iowa, and placed him under arrest for multiple murders. Brent Cooper, the district attorney general of the 22nd Judicial District in Tennessee announced the arrest later that day, revealing that Baldwin was the main suspect in three cold cases, one in Spring Hill Tennessee, and two in Wyoming. Baldwin is suspected of the 1991 murder of Pamela Rose Aldridge McCall and her unborn baby, and the 1992 murders of Bitter Creek Betty and the I-90 Jane Doe and her unborn baby. He was charged in Tennessee with two counts of murder in the case of McCall and her unborn baby. Two murder charges were also brought against him in Wyoming for the murder of the two Jane Does, Bitter Creek Betty and the I-90 Jane Doe, who had been discovered 400 miles apart in 1992. Baldwin, who grew up in Nashua, Iowa, graduated from Nashua-Plainfield High School in 1979. As an adult, he was a resident of a few different towns, including Nashua, Missouri, Waterloo, Virginia, Newport News, and Springfield. He worked as a long-haul trucker for Marten Transport for a number of years, spanning the times and locations of the murders.

Baldwin's arrest came as a surprise to friends and neighbors, many of whom described him as a quiet person, with one person going as far as stating that he was a "gentle giant." After his career as a long haul trucker in the 1990s, he moved to Newport News, Virginia, where he began driving a taxi for the Orange Cab Company. Here he met Edwards Huddleston, who was more than flabbergasted when she heard that her friend of over 12 years had been arrested for murder. According to Huddleston, Baldwin was a generous soul who was not capable of causing anyone harm. She said, "It just doesn't make sense to me at all. If this is true, it scares me to death to think I had my baby living there." She met Baldwin when she started working at Orange Cab Co., "He was the first one to come up and talk to me, and he and I developed a great friendship. He was kind of like my mentor."

The friendship carried on well after Baldwin had moved back to Iowa after losing his driver's license. Huddleston maintained that Baldwin was a kind a generous man who had helped her and her young family during their time of need. When her son was just one year old, she and her boyfriend had fallen on hard times, and were searching for a place to stay. According to her, Baldwin was their savior, offering them his home without questions, and then letting them stay until they got back on their feet. She described the two to three months of living with Baldwin as normal, and that he was a creature of habit. After driving his cab all day, he would come home in the evening with pizza and spend his time in front of the TV with them before going to sleep. Huddleston maintained: "Clark is the kind of person that if you are in need, he's going to help you. If he's your friend, he's going to help you." This makes it difficult for her to understand how this same man could be responsible for the deaths of three women: "I know him. If he was a serial killer, he had every opportunity in the world to take me out. If he was going to hurt anybody, I feel like it would have been me. Because I had thrown some fits in front of him in his own house. He'd get upset, you could tell he was upset, but he'd just go to calming me down, not aggressive toward me."

While Huddleston spoke to Baldwin's kind and caring nature, not everyone agreed with her. Baldwin was in a relationship with Rochelle Bobenmoyer, who had five children. Bobenmoyer and Baldwin married in December 1987, but the marriage was rocky at best, and the two got divorced in August 1988. Bobenmoyer's daughter, 37-year-old Jamie Jones, painted a very different picture of Baldwin. From age 3 to 6, Jones and her family lived with Baldwin, and her experience with him was less than stellar. She recalls the abuse she and her siblings suffered at his hands: "He would beat us with belts, and it would be on our bare butts. He would hold our heads underwater in the bathtub. That's just some of the discipline he'd do to us, and there were five kids."

Criminal Record

In 1991, a 21-year-old woman reported to authorities that she had been sexually assaulted while she was in Wheeler County, Texas. She stated that she had been hitchhiking at the time, and that she had been held at gunpoint. According to her statement, her attacker had struck her on the head before he bound her mouth and hands. She revealed that the man had raped her, and that he had also tried to choke her to death. She identified Baldwin as the attacker, and he was arrested and charged with raping the woman at gunpoint. When he was brought in for questioning, Baldwin admitted to the investigators that he had committed the crime. He was kept in custody until the grand jury was scheduled. Before the hearing began, Baldwin was released, and expected to show up once the grand jury convened. This was not to be. The victim disappeared without a trace, and investigators were unable to track her down for the hearing. They figured that since she was hitchhiking at the time of the crime, she must have skipped town with no intention of coming back for the hearing. Without the victim's testimony, the prosecutors decided to drop the case against Baldwin. This would not be the last time his name would appear in connection with a crime.

In 1992, Bobenmoyer, Baldwin's ex-wife, went to police to report a crime. She was short on details, and it was unclear whether it was actually a real crime or empty words her former husband was spewing to scare her. Bobenmoyer told authorities that Baldwin had bragged about "killing a girl out West by strangulation and throwing her out of his truck." These details were logged by the authorities, but the subsequent investigation did not reveal anything pertinent. Baldwin's name was recorded as a person of interest, with investigators hoping to figure out which case this "confession" matched up to. Bobenmoyer's account was vague and missed important details, so Baldwin was able to talk his way out of the mess with minimal effort.

However, Baldwin's next run-in with the law was more of an open and shut case that bought him some time in jail. In 1997, the Secret

Service received a tip that Baldwin was creating counterfeit U.S. currency on his personal computer. After validating the lead, agents were able to secure a search warrant for Baldwin's home in Springfield, Missouri. They raided the home, and this resulted in the arrest of Baldwin and two female associates. He was indicted on counterfeiting charges, and he served an 18-month sentence for the crime. He was released in 1999.

Until his recent arrest, Baldwin had not been on the radar of investigators handling the three murder cases.

Pamela Rose Aldridge McCall

At around 12:30 p.m. on March 30, 1991, a call came into the Spring Hill Police Department. The caller informed the dispatcher that a naked body of an adult female was lying at the Saturn Parkway near the off ramp for Port Royal Road. When police responded to the scene, they found the naked body of a Caucasian female at the wood line, about 100 feet from Saturn Parkway, and next to the westbound lane. After a quick perusal of the scene, it seemed clear to investigators that where the body had been found was not where she was killed. The woman's clothing was torn, and the undergarments were shredded. There were visible injuries to her face and neck. The evidence was logged, and the body taken to the Medical Examiner's office for an autopsy. Her fingerprints were collected, and investigators ran them in the system. They received a positive identification. The victim was 33-year-old Pamela Rose Aldridge McCall, and records showed that she was from Topping, Virginia. As they waited for the autopsy results, investigators began looking for suspects during their interviews. All they came up with was that McCall had been traveling with a truck driver. A number of witnesses stated that they had seen McCall at a truck stop with the driver of the semi-truck a few days earlier. No witnesses were able to describe the truck or the driver, or any details that would help the investigators point to a particular suspect. When the autopsy results were finally revealed, investigators were horrified to discover that there was a second victim: McCall had been 24 weeks pregnant at the time of her death. The medical examiner concluded that the cause of death was strangulation. With the state of her clothing and undergarments, the investigators were convinced that McCall had possible been raped and then killed to stop her from identifying her attacker later on. The torn clothing and undergarments were sent to a forensics lab for examination, and a semen sample was recovered from the pantyhose she had been wearing. Despite investigators quickly launching an investigation in McCall's murder, the case quickly went cold.

Bitter Creek Betty

On Sunday March 1, 1993, at around 4:30 p.m., Barbara Leverton was driving her truck along Interstate-80 in Sweetwater, Wyoming, when she decided to pull into a layby near Bitter Creek. She needed a coffee break, and was looking to change her fuel tank before carrying on with her journey. Clasping the steaming cup of coffee in her hands, she took a look around the stop. At the bottom of a snow embankment, she saw what looked like garbage. While she was not looking to clean any other person's mess, her curiosity got her walking towards the garbage bags. When she got close enough, she quickly realized that she was looking at something substantially more gruesome. At the bottom of the embankment was the naked body of a white female, completely frozen over. She made her way back to the truck and radioed another trucker. She explained what she had found and where she was, and then asked him to reach out to the police since she did not see any phones nearby. The Sweetwater Police Department received the call and investigators were promptly dispatched to the scene, where they found Leverton waiting for them. She pointed them in the direction of the body, and investigators immediately had a number of thoughts cross their mind about the body's location and discovery.

After noting the position of the body, investigators became convinced that the woman had been thrown out of a vehicle that was likely traveling westbound on the highway. The body had rolled down the embankment and come to a stop where it was found. The minimal evidence at the scene made it clear to the investigators that this was not the scene of the crime. An initial investigation of the body told investigators that the body had been at the scene for quite a while. The body was completely frozen, and with the brutal winter months that were slowly coming to an end, she must have been completely covered by snow for quite a while. They strongly believed that she was discovered because the weather was slowly warming up, thawing the ice. Fortunately for investigators, the brutal cold meant that the body did not decompose, and her face was completely intact. This gave them hope that facial identification would probably be possible. Knowing that this was most likely a dump job, crime scene technicians carefully combed through the snow hoping that some evidence would be discovered in the vicinity of the body. They recovered pink underwear and a pair of sweatpants near the body, but they could not be sure whether it belonged to the victim yet. The victim's body was then transported to the medical examiner's office. Having found nothing to help identify the victim at the scene, investigators made this their highest priority. At the medical examiner's office, the victim's fingerprints were taken and passed on to investigators. The prints were submitted to the FBI database, but no matches were found. They were then submitted to all state-level agencies in North America, but this quickly proved to be a dead end. Investigators turned their attention to the victim's facial identity. They figured that putting her face out there would be their best chance at identifying who she was. Flyers were created using reconstructions done by Carl Koppelman, Charles E. Holt and Wesley Neville. Investigators then contacted media all over the United States, and sent them a picture of the victim, now nicknamed "Bitter Creek Betty."

The medical examiner began his post-mortem examination, noting that the victim had been dead for a couple of months. He concluded that she may have died between 1 and 5 months ago, putting her time of death from October 1991 to February 1992. She had multiple injuries on her body, and she showed signs of strangulation. Her face and jaw had serious injuries, and the medical examiner determined that she had also been brutally raped and sodomized. However, the official cause of death was noted as homicide by stabbing. The medical examiner's conclusion was that Bitter Creek Betty had been killed by an icepick or a similar instrument. It had been inserted into her left nostril, and it penetrated her sphenoid bone. She was dead a few seconds later. Investigators were getting nowhere with the identity search, and no missing reports featured a woman with similar descriptions. Bitter Creek Betty was 5ft 8in in height, and weighed between 125 and 130 pounds. The initial DNA analysis concluded that she was of Native American descent, with collar-length dark brown or black hair, and black or brown eyes. Investigators were convinced that she was a mother, as the medical examiner had noted the vertical caesarean scar on her abdomen. She also had a one-inch long scar on her left calf, and a rose tattoo on her right breast. The tattoo earned her a new nickname, "Rose Doe." The medical examiner also noted that she had had some dental work done, but was unable to provide any more specifics. While she had been found nude, she still had jewelry on, a gold colored necklace and a plain gold band on her left ring finger. Investigators wondered whether it was a wedding ring. The investigators' determined that the perpetrator had Type O blood.

Despite the extensive media cooperation, investigators were unable to determine her identity. Her DNA profile, fingerprints, and dentals were put on file, and investigators hoped to find a match. The investigators turned their attention to the rose tattoo on her right breast and this turned out to be a better lead. The tattoo was traced back to a tattoo parlor in Tucson, Arizona. The parlor was located close to the Triple T Truck Stop. Investigators interviewed a number of people working at the parlor, but the information they received was not enough to track down the woman's identity. Just to cover their bases, the investigators asked the man who tattooed Bitter Creek Betty if he was willing to undergo hypnosis. He agreed, but there wasn't much to be recovered from his memories. He remembered her, but all he knew was that she was a transient, and that she was hitchhiking at the time. He revealed that she did not have any prominent accent, but that she did not reveal her identity. With no other leads, investigators hit a dead end. Her body was buried in an unmarked grave at the Rest Haven Memorial Gardens in Rock Springs, Wyoming.

Sheridan County Jane Doe

On the afternoon of Monday April 13, 1992, six weeks after Bitter Creek Betty's body was discovered, highway workers found the partially decomposed body of a female in a southbound barrow ditch. The body was found near mile post 5 on the west side of Interstate-90 near Sheridan County, 5 miles south of the Wyoming/Montana border. The Sheridan County Police Department dispatched investigators to the scene soon after receiving the call. When investigators got to the scene, it immediately became clear that the scene was just a dump site, and that the victim had most likely been killed somewhere else. She was fully clothed, and there were no obvious signs of cause of death. After canvassing the area surrounding the body, it was clear that there was no evidence at the scene to help identify the victim. The remains were transported to the medical examiner's office for a post-mortem analysis. The victim's fingerprints were taken and sent off to the detectives working on the case. The medical examiner estimated her time of death, and based on the level of decomposition, concluded that she had died sometime in February 1992. The official cause of death was blunt force trauma to the head. The autopsy revealed that she appeared to have been sexually assaulted, and they took a swab, but the quality of the DNA sample was not enough to enter into the state or national DNA databases. The medical examiner noted the injuries she had sustained to her body, and found that they were consistent with a brutal beating. Investigators ran her fingerprints, but there were no matches. They scoured through the missing persons databases, but were unable to find any report matching the victim's description. There was DNA evidence recovered from the victim's body, but there were no hits in the system. With her identity still unknown, she was referred to as "Sheridan County Jane Doe," and some also called her the "I-90 Jane Doe."

A profile was generated to try and identify her, complete with a reconstructed image of what she looked like. She was a Caucasian female around 5ft 5in or 5ft 6in tall. She weighed around 110 to 115 pounds, and had brown straight-to-wavy shoulder length hair that was sun bleached. Due to the level of decomposition, the medical examiner was unable to determine the victim's eye color. This also made it impossible to identify any distinguishing marks that would help investigators determine who she was. At the time of the discovery, she was wearing a blue and white mid riff checkered shirt with ties across her upper abdomen. The shirt had fancy pearl and false jeweled buttons. Under the shirt, she was wearing a size 38C light blue lace bra. She had on a size 5-6 blue pair of jeans, which was secured with a wide white plastic belt with a silver buckle. She was wearing pink nylon paisley-design bikini underwear. No shoes or socks were ever recovered. The only jewelry she had on was a pair of brass sphere post style earrings. With no witnesses or leads, the case quickly went cold. Her DNA, dentals, and fingerprints were put on file for future comparison.

Sheridan County Jane Doe was buried in an unmarked grave at the Rest Haven Memorial Gardens in Rock Springs, Wyoming.

Cold Case Investigation

Perhaps one of the greatest challenges faced by investigators working on the Bitter Creek Betty and Sheridan County Jane Doe cases was that Wyoming County law enforcement officials are not required to report the unidentified remains or missing persons to any state or national agencies. The county coroner's office is tasked with maintaining all the records. This meant that since the discovery of Bitter Creek Betty's body in 1992, detectives, forensic scientists, and officers have been unable to connect the dots in the case. However, in 2011, the details pertaining to Bitter Creek Betty's case were entered into NamUS – a system that contains the mostly scattered evidence involving unidentified victims, putting it all in a centralized location. The database then automatically checks for any potential matches in the case.

In October 2012, Steve Woodson became the director of the Wyoming Division of Criminal Investigation (DCI). Soon after he took the helm, he created a cold case unit which involved teams made up of FBI specialists and agents, DCI agents, and scientists from the state crime lab. Woodson's aim was to get a new perspectives and different eyes on the case. DCI Agent Loy Young's first case was the Sheridan County Jane Doe case. As he collected information regarding the case, he came across the DNA profile of the suspected perpetrator in the Bitter Creek Betty case. He reached out to a detective working on the case, and the two presented their findings to the cold case teams. With the drastic improvements in DNA testing, including ancestry and kinship analysis, and Parabon Snapshot phenotyping, investigators were able to determine that Bitter Creek Betty was of South American and European descent, and not Native American as was previously believed. The University of Wyoming performed further analysis on the Sheridan County Jane Doe's skull and mandible, and estimated that she was between 17 and 23 years, younger than was estimated by the original investigators. With no DNA matches in the system, the new investigation stalled.

In April 2019, the Spring Hill Police Department reached out to the Criminal Investigators in the 22nd Judicial District Attorney's Office about reopening Pamela Rose Aldridge McCall's 1991 murder case. The DA's Criminal Investigators had been handling cold cases since 2014, and had solved five by 2019. After reviewing the case file, DA Investigator Tommy Goetz reopened the case. He then sent the DNA evidence recovered in McCall's case to the TBI Crime Laboratory for analysis. The lab analyzed the sperm found on the pantyhose recovered, and submitted a DNA profile. The conclusive results showed that the perpetrator was a Caucasian male. The DNA profile was then submitted to the Combined DNA Index System (CODIS) database. The DNA profile matched the profile submitted by the Wyoming DCI in the cases of Bitter Creek Betty and Sheridan County Jane Doe. When the Wyoming DCI was notified of the new Tennessee match, they decided to team up with the 22nd Judicial District Attorney's office.

Arrest

As the new investigation into the three cases continued, the investigators sought help from state and federal agencies, including the ATF, FBI, US Secret Service, and the Iowa Division of Criminal Investigations (DCI Iowa). The investigators finally found a familial match to the suspect's DNA after a relative used a commercial genealogy website. As the investigators followed this new lead, they were finally able to identify Clark Perry Baldwin as their most likely suspect. He was a long-haul truck driver at the time of the murders, which matched up to witness statements in Aldridge's case – she had been seen with a truck driver before her demise. From February 2020, a Waterloo FBI taskforce began tracking Baldwin's movements with the hopes of collecting a discarded item that contained his DNA. Finally, agents were able to collect DNA samples and fingerprints after rummaging through his trash and swabbing items he had touched in a local Walmart. On April 14, 2020, the samples were sent to the Wyoming State Crime Lab for analysis. The analysis proved that Baldwin's DNA matched those recovered from the three victims. "The male DNA profile obtained from analysis of those items matched the suspect's DNA in the Wyoming and Tennessee cases indicating that the suspect and Baldwin are one and the same," the prosecution wrote.

On May 6, 2020, DA Criminal Investigators Tommy Goetz and Jeff Dunn, with the help of agents from DCI Wyoming, DCI Iowa, and the FBI, arrived at Baldwin's home Waterloo, Iowa, and arrested him.

Brent Cooper, District Attorney General 22nd Judicial District, Tennessee, wrote in a statement: "I would like to thank the Spring Hill Police Department for never forgetting about Rose McCall, and all of the investigators and agencies that have assisted in bringing this serial killer to justice. I am also very happy to be able to give Rose McCall's mother a chance to see justice for her daughter's and granddaughter's murders. As she put it in a recent phone call, 'At least I have a grave to visit, some Mom's don't even have that.' Now, thankfully, she has more than a grave to visit. As promised, my office will always attempt to bring those to justice who have taken innocent life; no matter how long it's been since the crime."

Pending Trials

Baldwin will be extradited from Iowa to Tennessee to face the two first degree murder charges in the case of Aldridge and her unborn child. Once the Tennessee charges get resolved, he will stand trial for the two murder charges in Wyoming.

House of Horror : The True Story of Rosemary West

14

Mary Gilmore

Unfortunately, it's not unusual in this day and time to turn on the news and hear a warning about a new serial killer roaming our streets. It's horrifying and hard to comprehend what could possibly make a person commit such heinous crimes. What is wrong with this person that drives him or her to commit such an act? The truth is that people have searched for the answers to that question for a very long time. Unfortunately, it still remains a mystery for the most part.

Rosemary West is one of those baffling cases. We will look deeper into her life and learn how her inner demons progressed to becoming one of Britain's most notorious and sadistic serial killers, taking the lives of at least 10 young women and girls.

Most of the information obtained by the authorities came from her husband and partner in crime, victims who escaped or were permitted to leave, and a great deal from her own children. Rosemary has offered very limited insight into the story, even to this day.

Remarkably, she did not act alone in committing these grisly deeds. This story is immensely complex, which I will attempt to sort out and then tie it all together with the union of Rose Letts West and Fred West in their vicious killing spree. There will be accounts of child abuse, rape, sexual deviance, torture, and murder. Rosemary West's crimes were so horrendous; it may be difficult for some of you to read.

Rosemary West's Early Life

Rosemary's mother came into her room one morning to wake her for school. Rosemary probably knew by the familiar expression on her mother's face that this would be one of those mornings that fills her life with constant dread. As she gets dressed, she begins preparing herself for what she knows is probably about to occur.

As she walks into the kitchen, breakfast is the last thing on her mind. Instead, she braces herself for the punishment she is about to receive. Don't misunderstand, Rosemary hadn't done anything wrong, but her father didn't need a reason.

His kind of punishment wasn't a time-out or a swat on the behind as most children receive. His were the kind that affect a child for a lifetime. Rose has no idea whether she is about to be beaten or if she'll endure other horrors that her father is known to inflict.

That is a likely scenario in the life of Rosemary West. Her father was a paranoid schizophrenic. The mental illness along with other problems, made life for her, her mother, and her siblings a nightmare. The abuse was bad enough, but what made it even more terrifying was not knowing from one minute to the next when or why her father's rage would erupt.

As a result of her home life, Rose made bad grades and became overweight. To make her situation worse, she was teased and bullied at school, giving her no relief from the continuous damage to her self-esteem.

There's a possibility that Rosemary's destiny was sealed much earlier in her life. It's not surprising that Rosemary's mother suffered from severe depression. The illness was so debilitating that she received electroconvulsive therapy several times while Rosemary was still in the womb, one of which occurred just before Rosemary's birth. There were some that thought this therapy was the reason for Rosemary's frequent outbursts of anger as well as her inability to do well in school.

Most of us would be unable to imagine a childhood such as the one led by Rosemary West.

Why do They Kill?

There are no exact traits of a serial killer to help us understand what drives them to kill. Some of them come from a two parent loving home while others have divorced parents. Some had abusive parents and others had loving parents.

Some think it's due to a head or brain injury sometime in their life; however, most people that have had brain injuries do not become killers. The majority of serial killers are men who act alone. Rosemary is not only a woman, she also had a partner in her life of crimes. Female killers and couples represent only a small percentage of serial killings.

The Federal Bureau of Investigation did a symposium, which was comprised of 135 experts who have dealt with serial killers in various ways to determine commonalities of serial killings. They determined that there are no definitive common traits. However, the central nervous system is constantly developing in adolescence, which determines a person's social coping system. That is, they develop the way they interact with their peers such as in negotiation and compromise. If it does not develop adequately, it can result in violent behavior.

It would be safe to say that the events of Rosemary West's childhood could be a factor in the choices she made later in life.

Rosemary's Life Before the Murders

Rosemary Letts was the fifth child born to Bill and Daisy Letts in Devon, England on the 29th of November in 1953. She normally went by the shorter version of her name, Rose. As we've seen, Rose's childhood was unlike most other children's. In pictures of Rose at a younger age she had an ever present smile on her face. You wouldn't guess that she was going through hell within the walls of her home.

The Letts family lived in Northam, a charming seaside town in Devon. Neighbors thought of Bill Letts as a nice man; however, they must have thought it strange that they rarely saw his children. When they did, the children were mainly seen walking around in their garden. One neighbor stated that they really didn't seem to be playing at all. They were just walking around and rarely seen outside the walls of the garden.

What they didn't know was that the children weren't allowed outside the walls and were afraid to play because they were forbidden to get dirty.

Although Rose's father constantly punished the children including Rose, he was not as physically abusive with Rose as with his wife and the other children. It was thought that he didn't physically abuse her as much as the others because he thought there was something not quite right about her.

Some people thought that he didn't hurt Rose as much because he was using her for his sexual pleasures instead. Others speculated that Rose learned at a very young age that she could control her father's anger by using sex.

Rose's mother Daisy, eventually left her father. She moved out of their house taking Rose and the other children with her, freeing them from the abusive environment. Remarkably, after a brief time, Rose moved back in with her father who resumed sexually abusing her.

One day, as Rose waited for a bus, she was approached by a man. Rose described him as a dirty man who had disgusting green teeth. She and the man struck up a conversation and even though his appearance was repulsive by most people's standards, Rose became attracted to him. The man's name was Fred West.

West was raising his daughter and stepdaughter at that time so Rose began babysitting the two girls. In addition, Rose and Fred also became a couple.

Fred's Early Years

Fred West, the son of Walter and Daisy West, was born in Much Marcle, England in 1941. He was the second of their six children. Growing up, he was considered to be a nice boy. They appeared to be a normal family, however, Fred's upbringing was perhaps even worse than Rosemary's. According to Fred, the motto around his house by his father was, "Do whatever you want, just don't get caught."

Fred would later reveal to police that incest was a common occurrence in his household. He said his father regularly had sex with his own daughters. Fred also claimed that his father introduced him to bestiality. In addition, it was thought that his mother Daisy took his virginity when he was 12-years-old.

Not surprising, Fred did not do well in school and dropped out at the age of 15. Two years later, he was involved in a tragic motorcycle accident. He received a broken arm and leg and a fractured skull. The head injury put him in a coma for eight days. Afterward, his family claimed that thereafter, he frequently become enraged without warning. Amazingly, two years later, he received another head injury. In this instance, he fell from a fire escape causing unconsciousness for 24 hours.

Fred's history of child abuse and head injuries would certainly coincide with the conceivable characteristics of a serial killer.

At the age of 20, he was caught and arrested for molesting a 13-year-old girl who subsequently became pregnant. He was convicted, but for unknown reasons he was not sentenced to prison. The reason is possibly because the girl's parents and Fred's parents were friends. Even with his family's propensity for deviant sexual acts, they had recently decided to try their hand at getting religion, therefore, they disowned Fred after this latest incident.

Fred had problems keeping a normal job. He landed a construction job; however, he was caught stealing. In addition, he continued to get caught molesting more young girls. It's amazing how he could still be roaming the streets even back at that point.

Shortly after, when West was around 21, he ran into a former girlfriend named Catherine Costello. She was better known as Rena, which was the name she used while prostituting and the name stuck. In addition, Rena was an accomplished thief. Nevertheless, even with her reputation, she was described by neighbors and other acquaintances as a very nice person and an exceptionally good mother.

Even though she was already pregnant with another man's child at the time, things heated up between her and Fred again and they married about two months later. The baby girl was born in February

1963 and was named Charmaine. Rena had another child by Fred a year later and named her Anna Marie. You will hear the names of these two girls in a shocking context later in the story.

Unbelievably, someone gave Fred West a job driving an ice cream van. This wouldn't seem a proper job for Fred the child molester to say the least. For Fred, it was the perfect job with young girls running after him. It was an ideal way for him to find victims.

While working at this job, a four-year-old boy ran into the street in front of his van and the child was killed. After this incident, even though the death was accidental, Fred feared people in the area would seek retribution for the boy's death. He thought it would be in his best interest to move away.

At the time, a woman named Isa McNeil was caring for the West's children. Additionally, Rena had become friends with a young woman named Anne McFall. They all moved with Fred to *The Lakeside* caravan park in Bishop's Cleeve, Gloucestershire, which is where Fred would later live with Rose.

With Fred's sadistic habits still intact, there were soon problems in this odd household. Fred insistently pushed his warped sexual necessities onto all three women. It became too much for his wife, Rena, and the children's nanny, McNeil, so the two of them moved to Scotland. On the other hand, the other woman, Ann McFall, had warmed up to Fred and stayed behind. Besides, she had already become impregnated by him.

Fearful of Fred, Rena and Isa's planned was to keep their departure secret from him and sneak away. Unfortunately, McFall told Fred, which enraged him. He allowed them to leave, but not with the two children, so the two women fled to Scotland. Rena returned frequently to visit her children.

After that, McFall began to pressure Fred to divorce Rena and marry her. Apparently, this didn't set well with Fred. When she was eight months pregnant with Fred's child, she completely vanished. She was never reported missing, but her body was later discovered in a field minus her fingers and toes, which had been removed and were missing.

Fred was left to care for his daughter and stepdaughter.

The Evil Duo Unites

Around this time is when Fred met Rose at the bus stop. It was at the time when Fred was caring for his step-daughter and biological daughter, so Fred already had at least the one murder of Anne McFall under his belt when he met Rose. Rose then began taking care of the two children.

When they first got together Rose was only 16-years-old and Fred was 12 years older at 28. Her father absolutely disapproved of the relationship. He threatened West that if he didn't leave Rose alone he would call Social Services due to Rose's young age. That was ironic since her father had been having sex with her himself for a long time. Of course, that was most likely the reason he didn't want her to go.

Nevertheless, Rose moved in with Fred and they lived together as a family with Fred's two daughters. After only about two months, they married she moved in with him at *The Lakeside Caravan Park* in Bishop's Cleeve, Gloucestershire, where Fred had lived with Rena and Anne.

Of course Fred, a man of few scruples, soon introduced his young and damaged wife to a sadistic world of pornography and urged her into prostitution. Due to Rose's demoralizing childhood, it didn't take a lot of urging for her to become caught up in his world.

Not one to hold down a regular job, Fred's contribution to the income was mainly by thievery. He wasn't very accomplished at that either and was frequently caught and arrested. It wasn't long before he was sent to prison for 10 months, leaving young Rose in charge of his two daughters.

To make matters worse, she had become pregnant and gave birth to her daughter, Heather, in 1970 while Fred was still in jail. Being young in addition to having mental problems, caring for three children was a tall order for Rose and she didn't handle the situation well, to say the least.

To add to the pressure, seven-year-old Charmaine, began to be unruly and Rose was unable to cope with it. Years later, according to the other child, Anna Marie, it was not unusual for both girls to receive severe beatings; however, no matter how bad the beating, Charmaine refused to cry. This infuriated Rose so it's no surprise that Charmaine didn't seem to be around any longer after that.

This is thought to be when Rose committed her first murder. Rose's tendency to lose her temper most likely caused her to loss control and kill Charmaine. Apparently, Rose hid the girl's body, because it's known that Fred disposed of the body after he returned from prison.

Fred would hold this over Rose in the future. On one of the occasions when Rose's father tried to convince her to leave Fred and come home, Fred made a remark that was something like, "Come on now Rose, you know what we have between us." For someone that didn't know Fred, it would sound like an expression of love. More than likely with Fred, it was his not so subtle way of saying, "You can't leave. I have too much on you." She later told her parents that Fred would do anything, including murder.

Fred's first undertaking after returning from jail was to dismembered and dispose of Charmaine's body. For whatever sick reason, as with Anne McFall, he removed her fingers and toes and then buried her. This became the normal process in Fred's body disposal. It was later speculated that Fred and Rose were possibly involved in Satan worship. It is thought by some that removing the fingers and toes of their sacrifices was typical for Satan worshipers.

The next time Rena Costello came to visit her daughter it naturally created a problem when she discovered her daughter's absence, thanks to Rose. As you can imagine, Rena was not happy about her missing daughter and demanded some answers. Therefore, Rose and Fred must have decided that Rena would have to go as well. So this visit to see her little girl resulted in Rena's demise as well. Minus her fingers and toes, she was buried in a field close to the Caravan Hotel where Rose and Fred still lived.

That meant a total of at least three people had already lost their lives courtesy of Fred and Rose West. One each for Rose and Fred and now Rena by both of them.

A brief time later, Rose gave birth to their second child, Mae. They bought a large two-story house in Gloucester; however, there was not much money coming in. Fred started putting up panels in the rooms to create multiple bedrooms called bedsits. They were tiny rooms, which didn't fit much more than a bed. They began renting out these rooms for extra income; however, the rooms served another purpose as well.

By this time, Rose's fulltime career had become *prostitute*. They also began working other women out of the house. One of the rooms labeled "Rose's Room" was dedicated to Rose for turning tricks. Outside the door was a red light, which was lit when the room was in business. The children knew they were not to disturb when the red light was on. The room also came complete with a peephole, which was Fred's method for watching his wife in action and for making videos.

Both Rose and Fred had come from a family where incest was normal. It was not unnatural to them when Rose's own father occasionally came to their house to have sex with her.

In around October of 1972, Rose and Fred hired Carol Owens as a new nanny for their children. She told her story years later stating that Fred and Rose attempted to bring her into their twisted lifestyle. Not wanting any part of it, she soon left their house.

A few weeks later, as she was walking home, Fred pulled up beside her and offered a ride. The next thing she knew he hit her on the head. When she awoke, her hands were tied and Fred was in the process of taping her mouth.

She was told that if she tried to resist, Fred would call in his friends and let them have their way with her and she would then be killed.

They said they would bury her under the paving stones outside their home along with hundreds of other girls. Terrified, she didn't attempt to resist.

Unbelievably, they allowed her to leave the next day and she proceeded to file charges on them. Fred somehow managed to convince the court that the sex was consensual. In addition, Owens decided that testifying against these two could be an unhealthy choice.

The couple was given a meager fine on a charge of indecent assault and then released. She would be the last victim that the Wests' would allow to leave alive.

Years later, she regretted not testifying. She felt that if she had, it could have saved the lives of numerous women and girls and she was most likely correct.

One day, Fred and Rose arrived home and their neighbor, Elizabeth Agius, was outside. She had become friendly with the couple, so Fred stopped for a chat. Just in conversation, she asked what they had been doing, so Fred proceeded to tell her exactly what they had been up to.

He said they were cruising around looking for young girls. He must have felt he needed to explain why his wife would go along with him on such an outing. He said they figured the girls would see Rose and wouldn't be scared to get in the car. She would later say that she thought he must be joking...he wasn't.

Meanwhile, Fred was busy redecorating the cellar. One of the prostitutes that worked in the house later told authorities that she saw black suits, masks, chains, and whips down there. Fred had created his own torture chamber.

Anna Marie, Fred's remaining child with Rena Costello, was the first to be brutalized in Fred's torture chamber. She was bound, gagged, and violently raped as Rose watched. She was only eight-years-old at the time and this treatment would continue for years.

Eventually, Anna Marie moved out of the house to live with her boyfriend, which quite possibly saved her life. Again, letting her go would prove to be a bad move for the Wests later in court. As one of the survivors, a considerable amount of the horror stories came from her.

After Anna Marie's departure, Fred's attentions naturally turned to his daughters Heather and Mae; however, Heather wanted no part of it and resisted. Understandably, she was unable to keep it to herself and told a friend about the horrors happening at home. This would seal her fate, but Fred later claimed to police that her death was accidental.

The life of Rose and Fred West continued filled with the unimaginable. They would go on to have a total of seven children who were born in a short time span. It is believed that three are by Fred, one is by her own father, and the remaining three are from her clients. It almost seemed that their reason for having children was so Fred and Rose would have someone to torture at the times when no one else was tied up in the cellar. You can certainly say with certainty that Fred and Rose West were definitely not loving parents.

The One's That Didn't Survive the Terror

Over the next few years, the abuse of the West's children continued as did the murders of others. At some point, Fred went to work at a slaughter house. It was thought that this is when his already violent habits became even more gruesome. It could have been a factor in his fascination for dismembering his victims.

It is believed the next victim was Lynda Gough who was a personal acquaintance of the West's. She enjoyed participating in some of their sexual activities by sharing sex partners with Rose. However, for unknown reasons she later vanished. Gough's mother came to the West's house looking her daughter and was told that she moved in order to pursue a job. While she was speaking to the woman, Rose was wearing some of Linda Gough's clothing.

Carol Ann Cooper, only 15-years-old, is thought to be the next victim. She disappeared while walking home from the movies.

Evidence showed she died by strangulation, was dismembered, and buried in the garden.

Lucy Partington was in town visiting her family and a friend over the Christmas holidays. She went to the bus station to take a bus back home and most likely Fred, being one to hang out at bus stations asked her if she wanted a ride. As Fred and Rose planned, it is thought that the only reason she let them even approached her was due to the presence of Rose.

It is thought that they kept Partington in captivity for about a week after she vanished because poor Fred showed up at the hospital about a week later with a large laceration needing stitches. Authorities think he received the cut while cutting up Partington.

Shirley Hubbard went missing when she was returning home from Droitwich. There was definitive evidence of her torture. Her head was completely wrapped with tape with only a short rubber tube in her mouth to breath.

Juanita Marian Mott was a former tenant of the Wests'. Her torture was obvious. She was gagged with a binding made of socks, tights, and a bra, which were all stuffed inside each other. She was also tied up with clothes line rope looped around her thighs, arms, wrists, and ankles. This was done with the rope going back and forth around her horizontally and vertically until she was completely immobilized. She also had a rope with a noose, which most likely suspended her from the rafters in the cellar.

Shirley Anne Robinson was one of the prostitutes that worked out of their house who had sexual relations with both Fred and Rose. She became pregnant by Fred, at the same time Rose was pregnant by one of her clients.

Shirley began to get the idea she would like to replace Rose, which is not advisable in this family. Rose demanded that she had to go. She and her unborn child were dismembered and buried in the back garden. The cellar was full of bodies by this time and the back garden became the new burial grounds.

Therese Siegenthaler was a hitchhiker in route from London to Ireland. Some of the evidence showed that like Partington, she was kept alive for close to a week during which time she was likely tortured and raped.

Allison Chambers was the last known non-related victim. She was killed in 1979.

Their oldest daughter, Heather Ann West, was the last known victim. Fred claims he killed her by accident. His story of the "accident" went something like this. He told police that Heather was being extremely insolent so he had to slap her. She then started laughing at him so he was forced to grab her by the throat to stop her from laughing. He said that unfortunately, he must have grabbed her too tightly because she began to turn blue and stopped breathing. He tried to revive her by putting her in the tub and running cold water on her, but it didn't work.

He then removed her clothes and attempted to put her in a garbage bin, but she didn't fit. Back into the tub she went so he could make her smaller, but he first strangled her with a cord to make sure she was dead. He told police he didn't want to start cutting her up and then have her come alive on him.

He also closed her eyes before he started cutting. He said he couldn't dismember her while she was looking at him. He must have been hearing a strange sound because he told police he found the source of a noise when he cut off her head. He said it was a horrible and unpleasant sound like scrunching. He also said that after cutting her up, she fit quite nicely into the garbage bin.

She was later put in a hole that the West's son, Stephen, had dug with the intention of it becoming a fishpond. Fred put Heather in the hole and built a patio over it. Stephen had unknowingly dug the grave for his own sister's burial.

Police also believed that they killed 15-year-old Mary Bastholm in 1968, though they never found her body. The Wests' son Stephen, later told authorities that he believes Bastholm was one of his father's earlier murders because his father boasted about it.

The Evidence Begins to Surface

Oddly, they violently murdered many of their victims, but then set others free after they had finished using and abusing them. Naturally, some of them went to the police.

The released victims were some extremely lucky women to say the least. Their reports finally got the attention of a Detective Constable named Hazel Savage. Savage was also familiar with Fred West and his arrests for thievery and child molestation through the years since the time he was married to Rena Costello.

Fred videoed an incident in which he raped Anna Marie while Rose held her arms. Anna Marie told friends about her home life who in turn told their parents. This and other information got back to Savage.

This enabled the Detective to obtain a warrant to search the West's property. It was the beginning of the needed evidence to finally remove these damaged and dangerous monsters from the unsuspecting public.

Fred was arrested and charged with rape and sodomy of a minor and Rose for assisting in the rape of a minor. Amazingly, Fred and Rose West were still not suspected of murder. At this time, the younger children were removed from the home.

Due to the evidence found in the home, Detective Savage had the suspicion that there was more going on here and she began digging deeper into this strange family. She had a feeling that there was something suspicious concerning the whereabouts of their daughter Heather and she was determined to find out.

For instance, it was noticed in the videos of the West's and their children that was seized from their home that Heather was never present. Also, in interviews with some of the children, they said something that should not come from the mouths of children.

Apparently, there was a common joke around the West house. Fred told the children that he would buried them under the patio with their sister Heather if they didn't behave.

Unbelievably, the case fell apart when two of the main witnesses decided not to testify. Detective Savage continued questioning the children repeatedly to no avail. Fred and Rose had programmed them and put enough fear in them by then that they would no longer say anything to help the case.

However, the evidence together with case workers reporting the family joke about their sister Heather kept Detective Savage searching. It also appeared that another child, Charmaine, was missing as well. Eventually, Savage put together enough evidence to obtain a warrant to dig on the Wests' property.

Soon after that, Rose answered the door to find the police with warrant in hand. She quickly called Fred to tell him the police were about to dig on their property and they're looking for Heather. It turned out that Fred would be of little help because it took him four hours to get home. He came up with some excuse about passing out due to inhaling paint fumes at work.

Could it have been that Fred was busy disposing of evidence such as fingers and toes or perhaps he had a burial he had not gotten around to completing. That will never be determined.

They began searching the house in addition to excavating the garden in February 24, 1994. The dig was originally intended to search for the body of the daughter Heather, which they soon found. Fred was brought in by the police for questioning the next day. He surprised the police by confessing to the murder of his daughter Heather and he repeatedly told police that Rose knew nothing about it.

Fred and Rose must have been up all that night getting their stories straight. It is thought that Fred assured Rose he would take all the blame and she shouldn't worry. Fred was good to his word, at least in the beginning.

Meanwhile, after the attending pathologist began inspecting the bones of Heather, he brought it to the attention of the police that there was an extra leg bone indicating the presence of at least one other body.

After that discovery, Fred decided he should do some damage control by telling police the location of Alison Chambers and Shirley Robinson's bodies. He hoped this would prevent them from doing any more digging.

It was first thought that Fred did this to avoid being categorized a serial killer, which is someone that kills more than three people. Unbelievably, as it turned out, Fred wanted the police to stop digging because he didn't want his cherished home to be torn apart any further.

Nevertheless, they continued and began to find more human bones. Rose was not arrested until around March 4, 1994. Even then, it was only for sex offenses. Fred had trouble deciding for sure if he wanted to protect Rose after all. He would go on the recant his confession that he killed Heather and then later changed his mind again saying Rose was innocent.

In Britain, prisoners are sometimes assigned an "appropriate adult", which is someone that assists and basically befriends the prisoner. This was normally done for juveniles; however, Janet Leach was assigned to Fred. Leach didn't know she was about to become the confidant of a serial killer.

It turned out that Fred became comfortable enough with Leach that he soon told her the whole gory story. She pointblank asked him if there were more victims. Fred responded that there were six more and went on to draw a sketch of his house and garden complete with the locations of the graves.

Fred knew exactly where they were located; however, he had some trouble remembering all their names. He recalled one that had a scar on her hand; therefore, Scar Hand became her name. Another he called Tulip because he thought she was Dutch, although she was actually Swiss.

Fred was now on a roll and confessed to the murders of his ex-wife Rena Costello and ex-lover, Anne McFall. He told leach that he dumped them nearby his childhood home. He then confessed that he buried his step-daughter Charmaine, Fred's child that Rose killed, close to the hotel where they lived in Gloucester. Strangely, Fred would admit to the murders, but he would not admit to the rapes.

Meanwhile, Rose continued to play the role of an innocent woman, denying any involvement in the murders. She went so far as to act horrified at the actions of her perverted husband. When Fred attempted to contact her, she snubbed him not wanting to have anything to do with such a despicable person.

After making bail, Rose moved into a halfway house with her son Stephen and her daughter Mae. The police were not convinced of her innocence and bugged the house. Nevertheless, Rose stuck to it and never spoke of anything that would involve her in murder. Only charges of sexual offense remained against her.

As can be imagined, the town of Gloucester was flooded with the media. The attention had a tremendous impact on the small town. The West's house became known by the appropriate name "The House of Horrors". The residents were in disbelief that this unimaginable crime spree had gone on in their town for 20 years.

The Trial

As it turned out, Fred took the easy way out. He hanged himself in his jail cell by tying together bed sheets leaving Rose to deal with the whole state of affairs.

She was finally charged with 10 of the murders since Rena Costello and Anne McFall were before she was on the scene. She went to trial in October of 1995.

One after another, witnesses took the stand and told their shocking stories. One of the highest drama moments of the trial came with the testimony of Fred's oldest daughter, Anna Marie. She was on the stand for two days. At one point she looked her stepmother straight in the eye as she told a story of sexual abuse and torture that began when she was a little girl of only eight-years-old.

She recalled the incident when she was so savagely raped by her father while Rose held her arms. During the incident, Rose was telling her how lucky she was to have parents to show her how to please her husband when she gets married. She said she was hurt so badly that she couldn't attend school for several days. She also recalled a day that her father strapped her down and raped her while he was home for a quick lunch break. These were only two of the many horror stories she lived.

The second day of her testimony was delayed for several hours because she took an overdose of pills the previous evening.

Another person that offered a wealth of damaging testimony was Fred's *Appropriate Adult* and confidant, Janet Leach. However, she became so stressed that she suffered a stroke during the trial causing another delay. It wasn't until later after the trial's end that Leach could tell police the entire story that Fred confided in her.

One of the key witnesses was Carol Owens who was one of the girls they brought home under the pretense of being a nanny. She was allowed to leave, but only after she endured their sadistic sexual torture. Needless to say, she had tales to tell.

Another witness who is still referred to as Miss A was lured to the West house and saw two naked girls who were being held prisoner. She watched as they were tortured and raped. She was then raped by Fred and sexually assaulted by Rose. She was one of the lucky ones that left that cellar with her life.

It wasn't hard for the jury to come back with a unanimous verdict of guilty on 10 counts of murder. Rose received life in prison.

The Aftermath

The "House of Horrors" at 25 Cromwell Street in Gloucester where nine bodies were found was demolished in October of 1996; however, there seemed to be a curse that affected many of the people associated with Rose and Fred West.

John West, Fred's brother, hanged himself while awaiting his trial for the rape of his own niece Anna Marie.

Anna Marie continued to suffer from the memories of her distorted childhood. In 1999, she attempted suicide by jumping from a bridge. She was rescued, leaving her to live another day with the memory of the horrors from her past.

Stephen West, the son of Rose and Fred, attempted to commit suicide in 2002 in the same manner as his father and uncle by hanging himself. However, it wasn't meant to be because the rope broke.

The actual number of murders will remain a mystery. During his interrogation by the police, Fred stated that there were two more bodies buried in shallow graves that they would never find.

He also told them there were 20 other bodies spread around in various places. He claimed he would show the police the location of one body each year. One wonders if he knew at that time that he would later take his own life and wouldn't be following through with that promise.

Fred took any other secrets he had in his evil little mind with him to his grave. After that, Rose wasn't interested in discussing the matter any further.

According to an article in the DailyMail, dated February 2014, even though Rose West filed for a couple of appeals after she went to prison, she has now decided she never wants to leave her top security jail cell at Low Newton jail in Durham and why would she, her cell is equipped with TV, radio, CD player, and private bathroom. She has never confessed to committing any murders.

Authorities know the women and girls were tortured, raped, killed, dismembered, and buried; however, they don't know the details of many of those crimes. Rose has been asked by numerous people to give those details, but she refuses.

Conclusion

This is an account of actual facts; however, it hard to believe that it's anything other than a fictional horror story.

Even after hearing about the disturbing childhoods of both Rose and Fred West, it's difficult to understand the extent of their warped minds. Even more disturbing is the fact that two people that are this broken can find one another and carry out their evil deeds together.

This story brings us no closer to the answer of what drives serial killers. Both Rose and Fred were abused as children mainly by their fathers; however, it was young women and girls that were the focus of their punishment.

There have been books and a movie made about them to show us how this horrific story unfolds. However, only in our minds can we come close to conjuring up the evil that occurred within the walls of 25 Cromwell Street. We may never know the full extent of the terrors that transpired.

The fact that Fred West is gone and Rose West will never see the light of day should make us all sleep a little more soundly.

A MOTHER'S KILLER : THE TRUE STORY OF JENNIFER BAILEY

35

AMBER ULLMER

Imagine coming home after a hard day of work through the door to your quarter of a million dollar home. Then, hearing an eerie silence and nothing but darkness surrounding every inch of your four bedroom, two bathroom, roomy home. With a passing glance to the dining room and living room of your 3400-square-foot house, you head up the stairs with the goal of taking a warm bath and getting a fresh set of clothes for the night.

This is what Susan Bailey[1] did just before it happened. Two dozen stab wounds and two slashes to her throat cut that goal short with a spattering of blood on the wall and a coagulating pool of blood beneath her. She didn't expect to be killed that night. Neither did she expect it to be her own children who would do it to her.

Susan Marie Bailey grew up as a bubbly, funny, outgoing, and smart kid, according to her mother, Kate Morten. She had curly dark hair, was the second of four kids, and was extremely musically talented with the violin and clarinet. Susan was always a people-person. She wanted to do something at the intersection of business, fashion, and people. So, she went to college and earned a business and accounting degree at her local Minnesota college.

To get her fashion experience, Susan worked at Levi Strauss & Co. while in college. She still wanted to get out there more. Her life was a struggle in Minnesota with the snow stomping on her every attempt to be successful. She couldn't make it to work during the winter and work didn't stop just for the weather.

Susan had a difficult time commuting to work. She had to struggle through twenty miles of snow and ice every day. Months and months of brutal winter weather created snow drifts and blinding blizzards that became a routine. She requested to be moved to a closer store which they allowed her to do. Even though it became easier because she didn't have to drive that far in that bad of weather through the winter, it

---

1.   http://www.apple.com/

wasn't any easier in the Spring. An extra 28 inches of snow replaced pleasant Spring weather.

Then, one time when she had to close up shop after the other customers left and the cleaning had been done, she locked the front door and discovered an empty parking lot. Well, almost empty. Snow took over everything in sight, including her car.

Snow chilled her to the bone, darkness swallowed the town, and she was all alone. The snow was so high that she couldn't even open the doors to her car to get inside. So, she called her parents from a pay phone in a state of panic. She cried and in a fit of shivering from the cold she told her mother, "I'm never going to spend another winter in Minnesota." She did just that.

With that, Susan moved to California and built a successful clothing store. Then, she met her husband, Richard Bailey. Not so long after, she called up her mom with a startling message. "Mom, I'm married," Susan told her mother over a phone call in 1988, "Richard and I eloped."

Richard worked in the military and Susan was forced to follow him around while he was in the military. After he finished with the military, he took over caring for his kids and Susan worked. She worked extremely hard and took good care of her kids: Jennifer and David.

She worked two jobs to make sure that her kids could have anything and everything they ever wanted. Problems started when Jennifer was 18 and she wanted a 16-year-old guy named Paul Henson Jr. He was into Satanism, songs about death, and role-playing games. Of course, Jennifer's mother wasn't so thrilled about this and forbid her daughter to see the boy.

Similarly, 14-year-old Merrilee White wanted to be with Jennifer's boyfriend and she was willing to go to great lengths to do so. Her mother, Amy White, also didn't like Paul and told her not to see him. Meanwhile, little David Bailey just wanted to make his sister happy who oftentimes had to take care of him because the mom worked so much.

According to Donna Fielder, author of "Ladykiller," Paul Henson convinced the two that he had two personalities. Apparently, each girl was dating one of them.

Jennifer was scheduled to begin at an art college in a few days and the other three were supposed to start at Northwest Independent School District. Under the veil of appearing to be innocent teenagers, the four of them plotted for days. They planned on killing their parents so they could all be together, drive to Canada, and live happily ever after.

Paul, a 16-year-old with a double personality in which one was an executioner from the 18th century, had been dying to kill someone anyway. He wanted to know what it was like. So, Merrilee attempted to stab her sleeping mother who luckily talked her out of trying to stab her, Paul waited at home with a gun for his parents, and Jennifer Bailey waited at home for her hard-working mom to get home so she could kill her.

Jennifer Bailey was the only successful one out of the three. Susan Bailey was just coming home after leaving her second job in Fort Worth, Texas for the day. She returned home just in time. Jen, Paul, and David took turns stabbing Susan 26 times[2] in the throat after Paul's attempt to kill his parents didn't work.

On September 29, 2008, 11:31 AM, it was reported that 43-year-old Susan Bailey was found dead in her Roanoke home. The Tarrant County Medical Examiner's office claimed that she had multiple stab wounds to her neck. According to star-telegram.com[3], "Sgt. Chris Almonrode said officers had visited her home in the 200 block of Oxford Drive on Friday at the request of the woman's mother, who had grown concerned after not hearing from her daughter. He said

---

2.　　http://donnakayefielder.blogspot.com/

3.　　http://star-telegram.com/

officers could not get an answer at the door and found no evidence indicating that anything was wrong."

Kate Morten, Susan's mother, tried calling her daughter from her home in Minnesota. When no one answered, she called the Roanoke, Texas police. No one came to the door of their upscale home, so the Roanoke police burst into the door and found a murder scene.

They found the mother's body upstairs in the hallway sitting in a pool of her own blood. Foul play was immediately suspected as the cause of death. The Texas officers also found a bowl of poisoned pudding, a chunk of hair, and an electrical cord dangling right into a bathtub. Inside the bathtub sat three phones and a knife under a foot of water. Jennifer and David were going to kill their mother one way or another.

Meanwhile, a curious South Dakota cop [4]stopped Susan's car for violating town curfew and couldn't believe what he found. He pulled over Jennifer Bailey, 14-year-old David, and 16-year-old Paul in Susan's 2002 Saturn. He pulled them over at a closed gas station where they were trying to steal gas. They didn't have any money and their stories didn't make much sense. They had no real plan either.

He took them to the station and called the police in Roanoke, Texas. They knew about the kids and the woman that the car was registered to. The Tuesday before that week, Paul's father reported him a runaway and thought he was at Jennifer's house. The officers did not find him there. They did find his packed bags and a driver's license. Later on that day, they came back when Susan found a loaded magazine for a pistol, but the police couldn't find the gun.

Roanoke officers quickly put the pieces together after hearing that the three were together in Susan's car. At first, they didn't go straight in when the mother called worried about Susan because no one came to the door and the car was gone. When they found out about the kids,

---

4.   http://www.apple.com/

that's when they went in through the house through a window and found the dead mother.

The officer called Roanoke police and upon hearing what was happening, he held the three on suspicion of capital murder. They were all held at a juvenile detention facility in Sioux Falls, S.D.

Paul wasn't able to kill his parents, they decided to stay out late for a dinner and a movie, thankfully. Merrilee White, on the other hand, didn't get to kill her mother Amy White because luckily, she woke up before she could. The 15-year-old Fort Worth girl was detained on the 23rd of September after her mother reported that she woke up and found the girl standing over her with a knife. Merrilee was demanding that Amy give her her car keys. The girl later admitted to the police that she wanted to take her mother's car so that could take her friends to Canada.

When authorities went to investigate[5], they found notebooks, binders, and handwritten papers, computers, and discs that police described as, "pertaining to the preparation of murder." In the boyfriend's home, they found handwritten notes, papers, computers, discs, and "The Demonic Bible." As mentioned earlier, Paul loved to practice Satanism and was fond of all the things any parents wouldn't want their 17-year-old to be into. He was an avid fan of role-playing and fantasized frequently. Only, this wasn't done as a result of the fantasizing mind of a deranged 17-year-old; it was real.

On September 23rd, police called the Bailey home because they were looking for the boyfriend who was reported as a runaway. Susan and Jennifer fought over Paul. Police later came back later when Susan reported finding ammunition. The police searched the home and found a butcher knife in between the couch cushions and a knife under Jennifer's bed. Jennifer was showing signs of plans to kill early enough

---

5.   http://www.nbcdfw.com/news/local/

Affidavits_4_Teens_Planned_To_Kill_N_Texas_Mom.html

that it could have been prevented. However, her sweet mother had no clue that Jen would actually kill her.

Their school district, Northwest Independent School District, commented on this in an article published on September 29th in 2008 at approximately 11:31 AM. They said, "Our thoughts are with the families involved, and our school personnel continue to focus on the education and well being of our students. Should any child or staff member need to talk about the situation, school counselors are available." Too bad their counselors didn't notice earlier how unstable these four children were. Susan Bailey might still be alive.

Donna Fielder, as mentioned later, spoke to Kate, Susan's mom, who said that she still couldn't believe that her grandchildren would do such a terrible thing. Kate lived through the moment with baited breath from the phone call that drew silence from her deceased daughter to the announcement that her grandchildren killed their mother, her daughter.

What happened to the other three kids? [6]Jen stayed in the Denton County jail without bail and the boys stayed at the Denton Country Juvenile Facility. All three faced capital murder charges. They even tried to try Paul as an adult. In this case, he would serve out his Juvenile sentence and then finish up his sentence as an adult afterward. Under normal conditions[7], juvenile offenders were released from Texas Youth Commission when they would become adults so they could serve out the rest of their sentence. Davide was tried under state's determinate sentencing statute.

Paul got 60 years in prison[8], Jennifer got 60 years in prison, and David only did his juvenile term then went on to live as normal a life

---

6.   http://www.nbcdfw.com/news/local/

Affidavits_4_Teens_Planned_To_Kill_N_Texas_Mom.html

7.   http://crimeblog.dallasnews.com/2008/12/roanoke-woman-indicted-in-moth.html/

8.   http://www.apple.com/

as he could have. When police asked Jennifer about her motive, she simply said, "We did not see eye to eye."

It seems like such a small charge for murderers. Would a life-sentence have been more deserved? Probably. Did they get a light charge because they were only kids? Most likely.

My Life of Crime [9]laid out the details in regards to the three murderers. Jennifer Bailey is a white female born on October 5th, 1990. Her maximum sentence date is September, 26th, 2068 which she has been sentenced to spend at Hilltop Unit. Hilltop Unit[10]. is a correctional institutions division (prison) located at 1500 State School Road, Gatesville, TX 76598-2996. It can be found three miles outside of Gatesville.

On The Texas Tribune[11], Jennifer Bailey is listed as being located at the Mountain View Unit for committing "LESSER INCLU MURDER committed on 9/26/2008 in Denton County" for which she is serving a "60-year term" beginning on "9/26/1008."

She is listed as a female, at 25 years of age, found in Mountain View under 01621147, from Denton county, and born 10/5/1990. She is white, 5 ft 5 in, 122 lbs, with blonde hair and hazel eyes.

Her parole eligibility date is 9/26/2038.

On *Denton County, TX Jail Records*, Paul Allen Henson Jr. is listed with the aliases of "Talos, Malaki, and Scai" with an SO# of 164000, and he is described as a white male with brown hair/eyes standing 6'3" at 145 pounds. He was booked at the Denton County Sheriff's Office on 06/09/2009 for capital murder by terror threat/other felony. His offense date is 09/26/2008. Because he has to spend 60 years in jail, he's looking to be released 9/26/2068.

---

9.   https://mylifeofcrime.wordpress.com/2012/12/07/kids-that-kill-jennifer-bailey-david-bailey-and-paul-allen-henson-jr/

10.   https://www.tdcj.state.tx.us/unit_directory/ht.html

11.   https://www.texastribune.org/library/data/texas-prisons/inmates/jennifer-bailey/727001/

A few years later, Candice Delong sat down in an interview with Jennifer Bailey for the details on Jennifer's perspective that night when they killed Susan Bailey.

During the video,[12] Jennifer says that she went upstairs and started feeling doubtful. She went upstairs to the bathroom and looked at herself good in the face. Jennifer knew she would have to look at that face for the rest of her life and the decision she was about to make.

She questioned if she really wanted to kill her mother. She explained, "That is when I made the decision that I was going to tell my mom what was going to happen and then call the police regardless of the consequences." She then said that she was too late. She heard a scream that broke her thought processes. She went out to the hallway and found her mother pushed up against the wall by Paul who had one hand around her throat and a knife in the other.

Jennifer Bailey then says that her mother told her to "call the police." She adds, "Then I said no."

Explaining why, she said, "Because, at the same time, Paul pointed at me and said, 'Don't!' And to this day, I have no idea why I said, 'no.' After I said, 'no,' Paul just grins and pulls the knife across her throat." From there, Jennifer and David helped finish the mother off. With that, they took off with the mother's car, no money, and whatever gas was in the tank to get them to Canada.

Donna Fielder, the woman who originally covered this story when working at the local newspaper in the Bailey's hometown, recalls the event in September 2008 that ended with the death of Susan Bailey at the hands of four teenagers. She explains how the four of them: Jennifer Bailey, David Bailey, Paul Henson, and Merrilee White tried to kill their parents and steal whatever money they could from them before taking their cars they planned on driving all the way to Canada from Texas.

---

12.   http://www.investigationdiscovery.com/tv-shows/facing-evil/videos/jennifer-bailey/

She recalls that the four teenagers plotted against Susan Bailey, a hard-working mother, and the long journey they made from her death to that run-down gas station they were pulled over at.

Jennifer Bailey, David Bailey, Merrilee White, and Paul Allen Henson enacted one of the most violent crimes in US history to a woman who did not deserve such an attack. It was such a popular case that filmmakers have taken to the story and made video-enactments of it such as *Deadly Women,* a series that took Jennifer Bailey's story and portrayed her as a young girl who fell in love with a pagan, Paul. Paul convinces Bailey to kill her mother and run off with him. They plan on running off to Canada together, but it doesn't quite go as planned. The mother tells her they cannot speak and havoc wreaks as Paul tells Jennifer that she needs to brutally murder her mother.

Susan Bailey was a hard working mother of Jennifer and David who had anything and everything they ever wanted until Paul came into the picture and what they had was just not enough.

Jennifer and Merrilee were bound so tight under the spell of Paul and David just wanted to make his sister happy. With that, they took a sharp blade and took away Susan's life and breath. They tried to get away and enjoy a happy life in the cold of Canada, but they lacked a plan and cash to make that fantasy a truth.

Perhaps this was all the will of a psychopathic teenager who thought he was two people. Sadly, he ruined the lives of two young girls and a young boy to fulfill his disgusting fantasies.

To this day, David and Merrilee sit alone and forgotten and without the ones they loved. Jennifer and Paul await 52 years more of time to stare at bars and cement walls. David lost a sister, a mother, and two friends. Merrilee lost three friends and the trust of her mother. Paul lost two loving parents and both his girlfriends. Jennifer lost the most: her boyfriend who she cared for dearly, her mother, and her self-worth.

The moral of the story? The all-American family, neighbors, children aren't all that movies and books make them be. Darkness taints the pages of every good storybook.

A MOTHER'S KILLER :

THE TRUE STORY OF NICOLE KASINSKAS

47

CHRISTINE GOODMAN

Nicole Kasinskas was a quiet, unassuming teenage girl. She was born and raised in Nashua, New Hampshire to Anthony Kasinskas and Jeanne Domenico.

"I lived with both of my parents and my younger brother until I was eleven years old," Nicole said. "And my parents divorced and my Dad moved out."

"I think after my parents got divorced and I was dealing with that, I became a little bit angrier. I had a little bit more resentment towards him, and it did change my perspectives about myself and about life in general, I guess even as an eleven year old."

In May of 2002, she found "romance" as a fifteen year old on-line with eighteen-year old Billy Sullivan.

Sullivan lived in a town called Willmantic where he worked as a line cook at McDonald's.

"Nicole hadn't had a lot of boyfriends," prosecuting attorney Kirsten Wilson said . "She was really caught up by the attention by this guy who was saying amazing things to her about how beautiful she was and what she meant to him."

They would communicate daily through e-mail, letters and phone calls. Despite not having met in person, they both declared love for each other within days, speaking of marriage and planning their future together.

"They filled in sort of the gaps of everyday communication and relationships with fantasies and making these assumptions on who the other person was," Wilson said.

"He lived in Connecticut and so our relationship was almost one hundred percent over the phone," Nicole said. "But it became everything to me very quickly because of the amount of attention that he paid me, and I didn't really feel that I was getting that from anywhere else."

Nicole had been vulnerable to Sullivan's Internet advances as she was a loner with very few friends in high school. She was routinely bullied at school by other girls. On one occasion, she was walking down the hall and one of her bullies had pulled her sweatpants down to her ankles. Nicole was not wearing any underwear, furthering the humiliation. Nicole refused to go back to school the next day after that incident.

"The bullying at school certainly made Nicole vulnerable to someone like Sullivan," forensic psychologist Fiona Russo said. "She's lonely, she's being picked on at school and completely humiliated. She stuck to herself and so when some guy pays attention to her, even when it is only online, her fantasy life goes into overdrive. She's able to project things on him that he doesn't deserve or merit."

The more severe the bullying became, the more Nicole began to withdraw and cling to Sullivan.

"As I got older, it was easier for me to isolate from people," Nicole said. "I think at that point I had just gotten used to being more alone as opposed to being around people. And it just became a part of who I was. Maybe if I was more open or maybe if someone had tried harder to reach out, that it could've been different."

Nicole's mom, Jeanne, was her best friend. Jeanne worked at an elementary school for a period of time, holding down such jobs as a crossing guard, a lunchroom monitor, and a paraprofessional for about three years before taking a job where she worked on group contracts for the Benefits, Brokers and Administration department.

"Jeanne Domenico was well loved in the community," Wilson said. "Hard worker. Really sort of a bright, energetic, sweet woman. She was trying to make her daughter happy."

Despite the bullying at school, Nicole got straight A's at school and made her mother happy whenever she made the honor roll.

"School really became my self-worth and I really identified with, like whatever my grades were," Nicole said. "However I was doing in school I felt it reflected on me personally, because I felt that it was so much a part of who I was. I never got in trouble in middle school. I never got spoken to. I never had a detention. It never really crossed my mind to do anything that would be against the rules."

"It would have been helpful if there was more of an acknowledgment that I was doing so well. I think it also would've been helpful if there was more involvement with guidance or something. Just more of a like a check-in...see how things are going."

"Somehow, someway, Nicole got lost in the cracks," Russo said. "That in no way justifies what she did. It may be how she justified it during this time. Her parents are divorced. She doesn't see her Dad. Her mom is working all the time. There had to have been days where she felt intense loneliness Going to school just to be ignored or bullied. To a fourteen year old girl you really may not see the light at the end of the tunnel. So you seek an outlet. Some turn to drugs. Nicole found her own drug in the form of the words that came out of Sullivan's keyboard."

MOTHER AND DAUGHTER TROUBLES

At least on the surface, there were no problems between mother and daughter.

Until Nicole ventured on-line and met Billy Sullivan.

Her mother found out about the relationship and wanting to make her daughter happy, drove the young teenager out to Connecticut so she could meet Sullivan for the first time.

"This was a two hour drive from Nashua to the place in Connecticut where Sullivan lived," Russo said. "It is easy to say here is where Jeanne made a fatal mistake. But in her mind, it is all innocent. Her daughter is fourteen and begging her to drive out to meet this guy. Begging and begging. Until she finally she relents."

More visits followed but friends and classmates knew little of the teen's relationship. Sullivan had informed some of his friends that he had a girlfriend that was "out of state." Other than that, he revealed very little about his personal life.

"He's quiet, he didn't really like to talk," recalled Danny Goss who was a classmate of Sullivan. "But he was good in school and didn't get in any trouble."

"I think the relationship intensified to a degree that Jeanne herself didn't anticipate," Russo said. "And it is easy to play Monday morning quarterback here but there had to have been some kind of father figure present to say 'hey, this is an eighteen-year old working at McDonald's. You are a fourteen year old honor student. You have a future. Don't blow it on this guy. But it isn't like teens listen to you anyway."

The two teenagers soon discussed the prospect of moving in together. Her mother quickly objected to this idea as well as nixing the idea of Nicole sharing a joint bank account with Sullivan.

But the young man later stayed overnight one weekend with Nicole's mother's full consent.

The relationship is the first for Nicole. She pedestalizes Sullivan as everything she has fantasized about is coming true.

"Nicole had a void in her life," Russo said. "When her parents divorced it certainly affected her psychologically in the way she viewed men. Then along comes Sullivan whose older and more experienced. She gets the love from him that perhaps she sought from her father. The older man, wiser than his years, showering her with attention. She was vulnerable to that."

"Her father didn't have too much to do with her after the divorce. She had that longing in her heart for that male figure. And along came Sullivan."

PERSONAL DEMONS OF HIS OWN

Sullivan, however, had his own personal demons he was fighting.

"He did have mental health issues," Wilson said. "He had been hospitalized a number of times. During high school he had some behavioral issues. Some anxiety, that kind of thing."

It was later revealed that Sullivan had been on numerous psychiatric medications to curb his depression, anger and schizophrenia. He had been weaning himself off the meds, however, and on one occasion he engaged in an argument with Nicole's mother over dinner.

Jeanne had asked Billy if she liked the dinner she had prepared. He said yes and then Jean made the comment that "I bet you don't get that too much at home."

Sullivan was highly defensive over anything that involved his home life. When Jeanne made that comment, he turned hostile.

"Sullivan was protective of his home life," Russo said. "If anyone insulted his mother or if he even perceives that someone is insulting his mother then he gets abusive. He did this to Jeanne, who had obviously made nothing more than an idle comment. That was the first warning sign and the relationship should have ended then and there."

Nicole, however, defended her young beau and from that moment the tug of war for her heart began.

"Nicole's own naivete comes to bore at this point," Russo said. "She has no experience with boys and here is this older guy that she looks up to, almost as a father figure of sorts, who turns her against her own family. Against the one person who loved her the most. Her mother. It is a tug of war that the mother loses simply because her daughter's hormones are raging and she doesn't yet have the emotional capacity to know any better."

After a year of dating, in August of 2003, Sullivan drove out to Nashua to spend a week with Nicole. By this time, they are both fed up with Nicole's mother's objections to their ideas of cohabitation.

"Our relationship was definitely emotionally abusive," Nicole said. "And I think now over time, from looking at it, my perspectives on that have changed so much. I feel like he is responsible for his actions and I am responsible for mine. I didn't really get that and I feel like in order to be emotionally abused, in order to stand for it and stay in it, there's gotta be something missing in you. There's gotta be something hurting already, something is not there, something's not right. And that needs to be figured out, found and fixed. Regardless of how a child is acting or what's coming off,there's more inside that kids need help with or guidance or just to have some type of connection with someone. You need to have relationships with people ahead of time, so that when the bad stuff does happen does happen you don't just come in to it expecting to work it out. Like, you need to have firm foundation with that person in order to work it out."

Nicole continued to side with Sullivan against her mother. The two argued constantly, Sullivan's influence quickly become apparent in Nicole's attitude toward her mother as she found fault with everything she did.

The two teens began discussing an unheard of option.

They began discussing the prospect of killing her mother.

"Well, this is where it starts getting...it's a scary business for me," Nicole said in a jailhouse interview. "I'll tell you that. I feel like I"m gonna cry. I don't talk about this stuff so this is really the first time. I think that my relationship with my mom was good. It was fine. I loved my mom. And...that changed. When...I'm not saying I stopped loving my mom, but...our relationship changed. I'm not gonna say that we were the most open because we weren't. We didn't talk about every little thing. I don't remember ever once talking about my parents' divorce with either of them. But the thing is, we didn't really talk about much of anything. When I was fourteen, I became involved with seventeen year old boy. This is really stemming into why I'm here (in jail) now."

OUT OF CONTROL

"Emotions begin to run high as Sullivan ups the ante in his hatred for Nicole's mother," Russo said. "Nicole is emotionally underdeveloped and has to choose between her mother and her 'man.' It is easy to look at it hindsight but with the teenaged girl's warp logic, she sees Sullivan as her entire world now. So she will do anything for him. Even murder."

Nicole's mom really didn't realize the danger that Sullivan was. She began doing what every mom does, demanding that her daughter stop seeing him, stop chatting with him and concentrate on her schoolwork. Nicole, on the other hand, remained fervent in her desire to move to Connecticut to move in with Sullivan.

"Jeanie, rightfully so, said 'you're fifteen you're finishing school,'" Wilson said. "'You're not moving to Connecticut' and that really upset both Nicole and Billy."

The prospect of not seeing Nicole had an adverse emotional effect on Billy.

"He started talking about killing himself...on the road...driving into a big truck because of leaving me..because of his sadness over it," Nicole recalled. "And I think now it just sounds silly, you know? But it wasn't then, and it was terrifying to me because I didn't...I didn't know how to...because of the way that our relationship was. Because he had become so much a part of my life. I mean, I really didn't feel like I was anything without him. I had nothing in my life at that time...I felt...at that time. So the thought of losing him in that way just wasn't okay with me. And that is unfortunately when conversations started about ultimately what happened. I guess I really I don't really go into too many details but I was sixteen and he was eighteen at that time. And I guess I should give you some background. He killed my mom and I was a part of it. I was not physically there but I knew and I helped him. I was, you know, going through the motions of what was being done. But mentally and emotionally, I don't think I was fully there. I don't think I was fully getting it."

"It was emotional manipulation," Russo said. "It is all so scary romantic for a fifteen year old girl to have some guy who is so in love with her that he is going to kill himself because he can't be with her. She has no one in her life to say 'this guy is a loser nutcase.' There isn't anyone that can talk sense to her. So she falls for the emotional manipulation of a highly disturbed but cunning con man."

Billy had convinced the depressed Nicole that her mother was an obstacle to both hers and his happiness.

"I really just did whatever I could to maintain that relationship because I didn't want to lose that," Nicole said. "I didn't want to lose him. And I quickly learned how it would go if I didn't always do everything that he wanted me to do. At that point...you know, getting to be fifteen...sixteen years old...I would fight more with my mom and there was a lot more to fight about, especially with, you know, this relationship that I was having with this kid."

THE FINAL PLAN

The couple tried different methods to murder Jeanne Domenico.

First they tried to poison Jeanne's coffee. The teens had placed Dimetapp, Benadryl and other drugs into Jeanne's coffee creamer in the refrigerator.

Jeanne used the creamer but didn't die and evidently remained ignorant of the plot on her life. The teens then added bleach to the creamer, wanting to strengthen the amount of poison. It was unclear in a court affidavit if Jeanne ever drank from the spiked creamer again.

The next idea was to set Nicole's mattress on fire with a candle. That idea didn't work because the bedding was made of fire retardant material.

It is unclear how the teens planned to fire up the mattress, whether they sneaked into her Nicole's bedroom and tried to fire up the mattress while she slept.

The third idea was to blow up the fuel oil tank in Jeanne's house. The teens had tied two ropes together which would serve as a wick. Their idea was to set fire to the rope which would then ignite a fire from the fuel tank. This idea was of course unsuccessful.

"These were hair-brained schemes from the start," Russo said, "particularly the fuel tank episode. What is interesting is that these are passive attacks. There is no face to face encounter with the mother, they just really want her gone. But it does show how these were test-runs of sorts. Sullivan was working up his nerve to do something violent. Nicole was building up her psyche. With each unsuccessful dry run, their determination and focus to do the job became greater until finally they realized that physical violence would be the only alternative."

THE ATTACK

The couple decided that Sullivan would do the killing. Nicole waited in the car at a local 7-Eleven where he mother worked part time to make ends meet. She wanted to wait there because she hated her home so much. Her boyfriend obliged, and entered the home of Jeanne Domenico between the hours of six and seven in the evening, waiting for her to come home from work.

The plan was for Billy to kill Jeanne by hitting her on the back of her head with a baseball bat.

Nicole waited anxiously in the car for an extended period of time then began to get worried as to why Sullivan was taking so long.

"Nicole called him and asked him what was taking so long," Wilson said. "Jeanne began getting upset that Nicole wasn't home and kept saying 'where is she? Tell her to come home.'"

Nicole heard her mother's voice on the other end of her cell phone telling her to "come home."

As became her habit, she did not listen to her mother.

"Sullivan did not attack Jeanne immediately," Russo said. "Again, he needed that fuel to add to his fire. So he confronted Jeanne, asking her why they kept refusing them to be together. Jeanne would speak logically like any adult would. She's underage. She's still in school. Of course, none of this would get into the head of Sullivan."

Jeanne made the mistake of turning her back on the young man. He then hit her across the back with the baseball bat.

"It looks as if Jeanne tried to get out of the kitchen door," Wilson said. "Billy started grabbing kitchen knives and attacking Jeanne with the steak knives from the state clock in the kitchen."

The attack was, in a word, brutal.

Sullivan stabbed Jeanne numerous times near her heart and stomach. He stabbed with such ferocity that the blade broke off the knife and he had to retrieve another. Then he stabbed her eight times in the throat.

"A number of the steak knives snapped off during the course of the attack," Wilson said.

According to later testimony by Sullivan, Jeanne managed to get a hold of one of the knives and tried to fight back. At this point, however, she is stunned and bleeding. Sullivan realizes that he is in trouble and goes in to finish the job.

Sullivan stabs her repeatedly as Jeanne tries to get away. A blade enters her lung.

"I'm done," were Jeanne's final words.

He then changed his clothes and cleaned the blood off. He then went back to Nicole, telling her to go inside the house to check for any weapons that he may have left behind. He also told her to get a towel.

The murder complete, Sullivan returned to the vehicle and announced that he had done the deal.

The couple, however, had a deal. It was now time for Nicole to do her part. She would help clean up the evidence left behind.

"The fact that she could go and clean up after Billy had killed her mother," Wilson said. "She had to have hit her mother with the door. And then she had to have stepped over her body to clean up for her boyfriend. That she was able to do that was chilling to do me."

Nicole took a cloth and began clean up her mother's blood from the kitchen floor.

"The fact that a psychopath like Sullivan was able to stab Jeanne to death isn't the most blood curdling aspect of this case," Russo said. "The really scary part is how Nicole was able to go back into that house, see her mother laying in a pool of blood on the kitchen floor, then begin to do her end of the bargain, which was to clean up after her boyfriend. The amount of psychological and emotional disconnect here is chilling."

The two then hid the evidence in the outskirts around town before going to a shopping mall in order for Sullivan to purchase new clothes.

Hours after the killing, Nicole finally began to realize the gravity of what has taken place. She realizes that she and Billy were not going off to "see the world." Her best friend, her mother was gone forever.

Jeanne's body would be discovered by her boyfriend later that evening and he quickly called the police. At around 10:15 p.m., Sergeant William Moore and Detective Shawn Hill saw Sullivan and Nicole approach the crime scene.

"They were cocky enough to think they could outwit the cops," Russo said. "By approaching the crime scene and acting all innocent, not knowing what happened, they thought they would deflect attention away from themselves. It really shows you how dumb these two kids were."

The police then stated the teens would have to be separated for an interview. Nicole protested, stating that Sullivan would not know how to get to the police station. The police informed her that they would take him there themselves.

"This is when things start to go haywire in their heads," Russo said. "Nicole is getting nervous, knowing that they will be questioned separately and face the prospect of not having their stories straight. These two were not exactly forward thinking individuals."

The two waited for the police cruisers to arrive and made conversation with Detective Moore. The detective noted that Sullivan did most all of the talking and admitted that he did not like police officers, stating that he had been charged before with crimes he did not commit.

Moore informed Sullivan that he would be given a "fair shake" in the questioning.

Sullivan, however, kept talking. He informed the detective that he had been shopping for souvenirs with Nicole that day and talked about Jeanne's relationship with Nicole. The detective said that Sullivan paced back and forth and then sat down on the trunk of his car.

Twelve minutes later, Detective Linehan arrived on the scene, making contact with both Nicole and Sullivan. Linehan noticed how nervous and "jumpy" Sullivan was. Linehan told Sullivan to "relax" and then the teen explained that he suffered from anxiety but did not need medication. He told the police that he had "no problem" to come to the station for questioning.

Linehan sat with Sullivan in the back seat of the squad car as they headed back to the station. Both of the teens were having casual conversations with the officers but after being questioned separately, they both admitted their involvement, leading police to the locations where they had disposed of the evidence.

"Both of the teenage lovers wilted under the police interrogations," Russo said. "She immediately ratted out Sullivan as the killer while he did the same to her. There was no loyalty for one another while under the police questioning."

Sullivan would be convicted of first degree murder, sentenced to life without parole.

Sullivan, however, did not let his Lothario ways go to rust in jail. He wrote love letters to a girl named Monique Teal who was then sixteen. This occurred while Sullivan was awaiting trial and later Teal's testimony was used in court.

Teal, using a pen name of Monique Sullivan in her love letters to Sullivan, had agreed to a date to marry the now twenty-year old murderer. Teal's mother, however, found out about the letters and forbade him to call or write.

"He just laughed about it," she said. "He said that no matter what my mom would say or do that nothing could keep us away from each other."

"You see him trying the same techniques on Teal," Russo said. "The immediate declarations of love. The flowery language. The idea of them against the world. In Teal's case, however, her mother put a stop to it."

Sullivan admitted to the Jeanne Domenico killing in one of his letters to her, Teal would reveal, although she didn't read from the letter in court. She said she obeyed Sullivan's demands and threw that letter away.

JAIL LIFE

Nicole Kasinskas would plead guilty to second-degree murder.

"My original sentence was forty years to life," Nicole said. "It is now thirty-seven years and a half to life based on a plea that if I acquired my GED I would get two and a half years off. I don't mark days off on my calendar. I don't do those types of things. This is my life now and I want to live it. I don't want to just look at it as one day down closer to my real life. Like this is my real life. I smile a lot and I live a lot and I'm happy a lot and I just prefer it that way rather than get lost in the sadness of it because you can. And I have. But if I...if I can choose not to...if I can be stronger than than then I want to. And it makes me feel freer. It makes me feel that I have more control of my life."

"Her life as a promising honor roll student at fifteen years old with her mother who loved her very much," Wilson said. "She lost her entire life. And for what?"

"I had no goals. I had no hopes and dreams, you know? You need to have your own hobbies and friends and stuff. Outside the relationship, there needs to be that balance. I just never had that, I never figured that out."

"Maybe if someone had said something like, 'I see you, I see that there's more to you than this and I want to see more of you. I'm here for you. I care about you.' I mean everyone needs help, everyone needs support."

BLACK WIDOW : THE TRUE STORY OF MARGARET RUDIN

62

BRIANNA VALDES

Margaret Rudin, dubbed the Black Widow of Las Vegas, went on trial on February 26, 2001 for the murder of her fifth husband, real estate king Ronald Rudin. After a lengthy, chaotic trial and her defense claiming that involvement in illegal activities resulted in Ron's death, the jury found her guilty on May 2, 2001. In August, the court sentenced Margaret Rudin to life in prison with the possibility of parole in 20 years.

According to reports, Ron Rudin went missing about a week before Christmas in '94. He paid a visit to wife Margaret Rudin's antique shop, in the same plaza as his real estate business. Officials said that Margaret Rudin did not report Ron missing until a few days after he disappeared. She told police she thought nothing of it at first because, aside from Ron being upset with her after an argument, he seemed like his usual self.

About a month after Ron disappeared, a couple of civilians stumbled upon human remain near Lake Mohave in Nevada. Police found ashes and fragments of bones in the burn pile. However, the skull, which was inches away, remained mostly intact. It had at least four bullet holes, which forensics later matched to a .22 caliber weapon. Police made two trips to the house, and on the second visit, they found blood on the walls, photographs and items removed from the house including a mattress and carpet. However, though the police suspected that Margaret Rudin killed her husband, the evidence up to that point was circumstantial at best.

A year and a half year later, a diver found a .22 caliber gun with a built-in silencer in Lake Mead. This was the same gun Ron Rudin reported missing about six years before his death. When officials tested the gun in the forensics lab, the ammo matched the rounds found in Ron Rudin's skull. Police determined that the .22 was the murder weapon, and, with this new piece of evidence added to the other circumstantial clues they had, charged Margaret Rudin with the murder of her husband. However, Margaret left town before they indicted and arrested her, and she stayed out of sight for over two years.

Almost a year after the diver found the gun that allegedly killed Ron Rudin, police finally indicted Margaret Rudin.

Authorities finally apprehended Margaret Rudin in 1999. Someone who saw her picture and story on the T.V. show "America's Most Wanted" called and reported seeing her in a small town in Massachusetts.

Police used a pizza delivery person to help them capture Margaret. They borrowed the person's uniform and an empty pizza box, and barged in the house when her male companion opened the door. According to some reports, they found her cowering in the bathroom.

Margaret Rudin was born Margaret Lee Frost in Memphis, Tennessee on May 31, 1943. She said that she and her family never lived in one place for very long, and that she and her two sisters constantly changed schools.

"I didn't grow up any place. We were constantly moving, you know, like, I transferred schools 22 different times, um, before I graduated high school. I lived in 15 states in 15 years. I never had a hometown."

Margaret said that her father was strict and dominating, and that he rarely showed affection to her or her sisters.

Both Margaret and Ron were married four times before they met at the First Church of Religious Science in Las Vegas. They married on September 11, 1987.

Margaret's mother, Eloise Frost, stood behind her daughter throughout the entire trial. She never believed Margaret capable of murder.

"I want to live long enough to see Margaret pronounced innocent, because she is innocent."

Margaret Rudin's daughter, Kristina Mason firmly believed that her mother was innocent. She said her childhood was a good one, and that the mother with whom she grew up was not a murderer.

"She's just a wonderful person and I'm proud to say she's my mother."

The court sentenced Margaret Rudin in September 2001. Although she received life in a medium security facility, plus a year for planting the bugs in her husband's office, they also added that she would be eligible for parole in 2011. She began preparing, and petitioning, for her appeal, carefully heeding the filing deadlines.

80-year-old Eloise cried when Margaret was convicted, saying that now she may never see her daughter again.

Kristina Mason burst into tears.

"I'm so disappointed."

Ronald Rudin seemed to predict his own death, or at least his murder. Months before he went missing, he had his will changed, with specific instructions for investigators to follow in the event that he died under suspicious circumstances.

"In the event my death is caused by violent means [for example gunshot, knife or a violent automobile accident] extraordinary steps be taken in investigating the true cause of the death. Should said death be caused directly or indirectly by a beneficiary of my estate, said beneficiary shall be totally excluded from my estate and/or any trusts I may have in existence."

Although most of Nevada's case against Margaret was circumstantial, authorities say there were a few things that seemed suspicious to them from the beginning. First, Margaret herself admitted that her marriage to Ron was less than ideal. She told police that they often argued about her work schedule. Later, when authorities discovered that she had planted listening devices in Ron Rudin's home office, she also admitted that she suspected that Ron was having an affair, and upon eavesdropping on a phone conversation, discovered proof to back her suspicions.

Jimmy Vacarro, a Vegas detective, confirmed that the Las Vegas police believed without a doubt that Margaret Rudin was responsible for Ron's murder.

"We know there was this real rocky roller-coaster relationship between Margaret Rudin and her husband... [It took] Margaret two days to file a missing persons report and that she did so only after Ron's coworkers informed police first...Generally speaking, the spouse is missing, the wife's the one reporting it."

Second, officials say that Margaret waited a few days before reporting Ron missing, even though his employees at his real estate company were concerned and investigating as soon as he did not show up that Monday morning.

Margaret Rudin offered a logical explanation to her hesitation to bring in police. She said she thought little of it at first because they had another fight and he left angry, which was common for Ron. She also said that, aside from Ron being upset with her after an argument, he seemed like his usual self.

"He seemed ok. He does not seem upset. He had, had been a little peeved at me over the weekend because I had to work all the time... "Well, I thought nothing of it because, you know, maybe he did get peeved... and maybe he did decide to go out for awhile... maybe he did go to, you know... wherever."

Margaret made a point of mentioning her previous marriages in one of her interviews.

"I don't have a history of staying with somebody if I'm really unhappy. I have a history of divorcing... There was problems. He was a difficult person at times, but yes, I did love him..."

Margaret said Ron also drank quite a bit after just a few months of marriage. However, she told reporters that she was not mad about the alcohol or the other women, even when Su Lyles, a close friend and a former employee of Mr. Rudin's, testified that in the fall of 1993, their relationship became more intimate. At least twice, she said, they had discussed their feelings for each other over the telephone during calls made from his office.

"You know why? It is because 99 percent of the men that I have ever had in my life had affairs. Ninety percent of men do, you might as well expect it."

Margaret admitted that, although the affairs wounded her, she loved her husband and desperately wanted to work out things with him.

Police grew even more suspicious when they discovered that Margaret hired a man named Augustine Lovato to help her remove some dirty carpet and furniture from the master bedroom. She then renovated the bedroom she shared with her husband into an office while Ron was still missing.

Lovato testified that the mattress and carpet he removed from the Rudin's home had suspicious brown stains on it and a strong odor that alarmed him.

"It didn't seem right, him still being missing and me turning their master bedroom into an office and then those splatters on that picture. Like I got the heebie-jeebies."

Lovato also claimed that he heard a strange sound in the bathtub in the master bathroom. He said that, upon inspection, it looked about the same color and consistency as the stains on the mattress and carpet he removed.

The same day he moved the allegedly bloodstained items from the Rudin's bedroom, Margaret Rudin asked Lovato to mail a package addressed to her mother. Lovato claimed that he forgot to mail the package, and ultimately turned it over to the police. After obtaining a search warrant, police opened the package and discovered several personal items inside, including a postcard from Israel signed "Love, Yehuda," a photo of Yehuda Sharon, the man with whom police suspected that Margaret Rudin was having an affair, and a handwritten letter from Rudin to her mother containing the message, "Please hold on to my Ye."

Attorneys discovered later that Lovato reported all these mysterious findings after Ron Rudin's other trustees announced their reward for information about Ron's disappearance. However, Lovato argued that he cooperated with police before anyone told him there was a reward, which Ron's trustees did grant him.

The most suspicious thing that Margaret Rudin did, according to police, was going on the run before the state served her with her indictment. Investigators believed that, if Margaret were innocent, she would not have fled. However, Margaret says that she ran out of fear, not guilt.

"[I ran] because I was afraid of being found by Ron's shadowy business associates... It was difficult. I was always looking over my shoulder. I was always afraid, I was afraid of who stood to gain the most, you know, from Ron's murder."

During the trial, the state also used the testimony of almost 70 witnesses, including Yehuda Sharon and Margaret's sister, Donna Cantrell. Prosecutors granted Yehuda Sharon total immunity in exchange for his testimony against Margaret Rudin. However, when he took the stand, he not only had little to say regarding Margaret's guilt, he denied aiding her in disposing of Ron Rudin's remains. He told the court that he rented a van, planning to make a trip from Vegas to California for his business on the night in question. However, he said that he only made it half way there and then turned around due to unexpected weather conditions. Furthermore, his destination was the opposite direction from the place where officials found Ron Rudin's remains. Once the prosecution determined that Margaret's friend, Yehuda Sharon, was likely not an accomplice to Ron's murder, no other suspects were detained or questions, and most people assumed that Margaret had somehow dismembered her husband's body, put it in the heavy steamer trunk and hauled it out to the desert all by herself.

Cantrell testified that she was aware of her sister's marital problems. She said that Margaret had spoken to her many times about Ron's drinking and her suspicions about his involvement with other women. She made comments on Rudin's restless desire to get away from Ron.

"I said, 'I thought you were going to divorce him,' and she said, 'He's not in very good health. He can't even walk without being out of breath, and I think I'll wait.' [Margaret told me] to tell [police] that she and Ron were getting along better than ever. And that the girlfriend wasn't an issue. [I don't] think that this statement would have been true."

Despite the authorities' strong belief that she murdered her husband, Margaret Rudin maintained her innocents. In interviews after the trial and her conviction, she states repeatedly that she loved her husband and could never kill him. She suggested that there might be another motive for her husband's murder.

"Nobody knows the whole Ron. That's the part that worries me. Maybe there's something that was going on with a business or a personal deal."

Margaret also suspected that someone knew more than they told detectives.

"I think that there are people that know things. I think that there are people who haven't come forth before. Maybe they didn't know how, maybe they were afraid, maybe they were intimidated."

Margaret Rudin's trial was rocky from the beginning. One of her defense attorneys, Michael Amador, started with an opening statement, which consisted of nothing but a long, irrelevant, self-based speech.

"This is a great day, in a lot of different ways. Some days are difficult; some days we hear bad news or we go through a difficult time, but every day, every day, depending on how you look at it, with a few exceptions, can be a celebration.

This is a great today for me. This is a culmination of a career. The people in this case, we are not strangers; we know each other. Chris and

I were sworn in as deputy DAs the same day. And I congratulate Chris on a presentation that was organized and well thought out, the best money can buy. It was really good.

If you want to know an opinion about me, I guarantee you'll find some, different ones from different people. Not many people know me. I have few close friends, like Ronald Rudin had few close friends.

I could be a wonderful, caring father, coaching soccer, helping kids with their homework, which I did the first time I got married when they were young.

Then another day, I might scream at someone, yell at them for-I don't know-for asking me some question, because I was too busy and I was thinking of something else.

The difficulty I have at times is communicating to people. I have to look at it and talk to other people and they will bring me back down to earth and say, Mike, what are you trying to say? What are you trying to get across?"

Amador also made a strange, challenging statement.

"During the course of the trial, there may be objections and things like that. Don't worry about it."

Judge Joseph Bonaventure cut off Amador's speech.

"I don't know what that means: Don't worry about objections. We have to do other things. I have no idea what that means. If there's an objection, I'm either going to overrule it or sustain it and that's the law... I keep saying this-and I let you get away with a lot, Mr. Amador-but the purpose for an opening statement is just to indicate what the evidence is going to tend to show and not go into your personal beliefs and your passion and soccer dad and yelling at the staff and whether you were a green lawyer and know all the cops and used to be a D.A. and you communicate differently. I never heard that in [an] opening statement in my life."

During the opening statements, the State quoted a portion of Margaret Rudin's diary.

"My life has always been unique, exciting, full of change, challenges and stimulus and full of interesting casts of characters and that is okay.

It just is, and I accept that for my past, but I know that, by programming my mind, I can now redirect any future stage plays and pick my own screen play and cast, because I am the producer, director and star of any and all new plays on my stage called life.

I've always vaguely known these facts and lived my life accordingly, but I never realized what control-I never realized what control I could have over every segment of this one time stage production called "Margaret's Life.""

Amador did a curious thing at the trial. He employed a makeup artist from a professional modeling agency and paid almost $500 an hour, out of his own pocket, to make Margaret appear worn, delicate, and tired.

Amador got under Judge Bonaventure's skin by repeatedly being late to appear in court, questionable forms he submitted, and his cell phone, which he never turned off or down during the trial. Rumors eventually spread that Amador was using drugs, drinking and partying all night long when he had to be in court early the next morning.

Rumors circulated that Amador was also behaving inappropriately with Margaret Rudin's belongings and private, confidential information. Amador hired a new office assistant named Annie Jackson during the proceedings for the Rudin trial. She revealed information regarding some of the rumors about Amador.

"There is no other way to say the following: when Mr. Amador told the court that he did not have any book or movie contracts, he was lying. Michael Amador does have book contracts and movie contracts regarding the Margaret Rudin case. When we returned to the office after Mr. Amador made those false representations to the court, he asked me to grab all of the contracts so that he could put them in his little safe in the back closet. He told me, "I don't want anyone to find out that I have these, then I'm sure they'll be investigating and looking for these."

Margaret asked early on for an even amount of participation from her attorneys. She asked that Thomas Pitaro take a more active role in the proceedings, because she did not believe that Michael Amador was properly prepared.

"We haven't even subpoenaed my witnesses yet. And I'm getting so nervous. I mean, I'm getting panicky."

Pitaro agreed after warning the judge that, although he would do his best, he was uncertain if he would be able to uphold that bargain throughout the entire trial.

Throughout all the chaos in the Rudin trial, one juror believed Margaret's side of the story. During the first couple of days of deliberation, she held fast to her opinion that Margaret did not kill Ron. However, hours before the foreperson read the jury's verdict, juror #11 changed her vote. She was distraught, wiping her eyes with a napkin. She hesitated before replying with a hushed "Yes" when the court asked her if the verdict was, in fact, hers, too.

Even though the verdict was ultimately unanimous, the juror cried as she apologized to Rudin when the foreperson read the jury's verdict.

During the time before she opted to vote Margaret Rudin guilty, juror #11 faced allegations from her peers of choosing not to join the deliberation efforts, lying, and calling one of the jury substitutes with her concerns about the case. Amador said he thought the juror was possibly "brow-beaten" into changing her vote.

Foreperson for the Rudin case's jury, Ronald Vest, said that no one "twisted her arm."

"We didn't bribe her or threaten her. She came to this on her own."

Vest believed that Rudin's was an open and shut case.

"Rudin's guilt was clear early on. [The defense's case was] a waste of time... [Amador was] bordering on incompetent... [The guilty verdict was a] slam dunk with a stepladder... I didn't buy any of it. I don't think any of us bought any of the defense case. The mountain of evidence had 11 of the jurors ready to convict as early as Thursday, but one person from the beginning did not see it that way... juror #11 seemed so bent on acquitting Rudin that [I] began to wonder if she had been bribed or threatened or simply wanted attention. [I] confronted her about [my] suspicions, and she denied them. There was a little bit of swearing. It was fast and furious but we hashed it out."

Vest admitted that he had had to request substitutes on a few occasions, because his special needs students were struggling in class without him. He believed that, had he not been there, they would not have been able to replace him.

"Six substitutes, three of which said they would never come back and one who just sat at the desk shaking like he was scared... my principal said, Well, maybe there's some reason why you need to be on this jury."

The judge in the Rudin trial met with the hesitant juror privately, in his chambers, to address her contact, and discussion about case-related information, with an alternate juror. Whenever Margaret Rudin's defense team broached the subject, the court dismissed it, stating that it had little impact on the outcome of the trial.

Margaret Rudin's conviction shocked Amador. He spoke with disdain about the prosecutors. He could not believe that the prosecutors successfully sold their case.

"If you have any understanding of psychology, history, or criminology, women don't do that, men do," said Amador. "That kind of mutilation is done by men over money or, in rare cases, serial killers. Women don't even order stuff like that—they want it clean... [The prosecutors] make me sick... I don't know how it is that right-thinking people can find someone guilty with no evidence."

Rudin had requested a mistrial due to Amador's antics and all the dissention with the jury. Pitaro led the defense team at the motion, hoping to prove that Amador was ill prepared for the case and not behaving with appropriate competence as an attorney.

"The fundamental problem that we have is this case is not ready to go to trial. For whatever reason it's not ready, it's not ready. That's obvious to any observer of this case, that for the first two weeks this is not the way you try cases and this is not the way you try murder cases. And what we are putting on in front of the world is a farce, and that disturbs me as an attorney. [T]his has become a sham, a farce and a mockery."

The State expressed similar concerns.

"Already we have an appellate issue now, should they have hired a forensic accountant. And I mean they came into this thing hiring their experts two weeks before the trial and they didn't start looking at the evidence until the day of trial. Two days into it, we still don't have reports back for most of them... Mr. Pitaro is coming in now, he's going to try to read the stuff and catch up. He already feels there's certain things that should have happened that didn't happen. All I can say is we're really uncomfortable with the record here."

The district court, however, was hesitant to declare a mistrial because of the double jeopardy laws. As it turned out, those did not apply in Margaret Rudin's case.

Amador stood with Margaret Rudin and the rest of her defense team during the motion for mistrial. However, when the prosecutors submitted documentation regarding his ineffectiveness, he contradicted himself.

"Nobody worked harder or spent more time before or during the Rudin trial nor knew the case better than I... [I] spend many hours on the case, from the time [I] took it in August of 2000 and [my] vacation in November 2000... [I] filed at least 24 motions and investigated all major witnesses in the case and organized their files prior to the vacation."

The defense also argued that improper communication took place between the judge, juror 11 and the alternate, which tainted the jury. According to the alternate, juror 11 called the alternate, saying she was upset because she was the only person in favor of a not guilty verdict and because she had gotten into an altercation with the staff person at a restaurant during a recess. After questioning the alternate and the juror in the presence of the State and the defense, the district court denied Rudin's motion for a mistrial. The district court also chose not to replace the juror. They concluded that neither the jury nor Rudin's case were compromised.

The court removed Amador from Margaret Rudin's case, but rejected her request for a mistrial. The judge almost immediately disregarded Margaret's mistrial motion.

"[Rudin] failed to present any specific argument to support a determination that she has been prejudiced. [The] affidavits are legally insufficient, as conclusions, rumors, beliefs, and opinions are not sufficient to form a basis for a new trial... As to Mr. Amador's personal antics which the defense seems to harp upon as tantalizing tidbits, this court feels it is not honorable to kick a man when he is down as the record speaks for itself. Rudin, at taxpayer expense, also had at her side criminal defense attorneys Thomas Pitaro and John Momot."

Bonaventure was biased, blunt, and cold at Margaret's sentencing hearing, just as he was throughout the entire trial.

"You're going to be locked away in the cold confines of your prison cell, never to be heard from again."

Although she received life in a medium security facility, plus a year for planting the bugs in her husband's office, they also added that she would be eligible for parole in 2011. She began preparing, and petitioning, for her appeal, carefully heeding the filing deadlines.

The appeals court believed that one of Margaret Rudin's former attorneys, Dayvid Figler, was responsible for her initial petitions for appeal. Figler denied any wrongdoing, and said that, although he was not at fault, she did deserve a shot at a new trial.

"I didn't screw up her trial. I didn't screw up her appeal. The court was giving extra time to get this very burdensome case before it. Everyone was operating under the assumption that she had more time to file the post-conviction appeal."

Figler called Rudin's appeal a "very complicated, burdensome, voluminous case" and said that after he took it on, the trial judge granted him extra time because the case was so complex.

Christopher Oram, the lawyer who represented Margaret Rudin during her recent appeal for a new trial, was thrilled with the opportunity.

"She is absolutely innocent. We've been working to prove it for a long time. I'm trying to reverse 10 years of complex litigation that was very unfair... I believe in her innocence. I'm ready to fight, and I wish they would stop playing their games. In the end, get in the ring and fight."

The Ninth Circuit Court of Appeals said that a technicality should not hinder Margaret Rudin's attempt to prove that a lawyer at her original trial ineffectually proved her case. Judge Mary Murguia believed that Figler did not serve Margaret to the best of his ability.

"While Figler regularly attended the court's status hearings, he appears to have done nothing else in support of his client's request for post-conviction relief. [Figler had the case for 645 days] and during that time, [he] had filed nothing in either state or federal court."

In 2007, Oram filed the first and only petition for post-conviction relief, according to Murguia.

Sally Loehrer, a district judge, ruled in 2008 that Michael Amador's performance did constitute as ineffectual in her original trial, and as a result, Margaret Rudin was entitled to a new trial.

"[It was a] case laced with intrigue and spins and loops involving a cast of characters and witnesses [that seemed to have] a lot of ulterior motives."

However, two years later, the Supreme Court overruled, stating that there was not enough evidence to sustain the order.

The Ninth Circuit Court reviewed all the evidence from the original trial, as well as Margaret Rudin's complaints, and her defense team's strategies. They do not believe that all defense attorneys adequately represent their clients just because they participate in every aspect of the trial. They made mention of evidence that was not previously mentioned.

"Sometime during the trial, the defense team located the person who sold the trunk to Rudin and established that it was not a large humpback trunk, but one that was much too small to fit a corpse inside. The defense also located Barbara Orcutt, who indicated that Rudin was indeed concerned about Ron's disappearance and had asked her right after his disappearance to organize a search in the Mt. Charleston area, where she believed Ron might have been. The State apparently had this information, but did not share it with the defense. It is unrealistic to think that the jurors could have put out of their minds all the evidence and adverse events, including the continual admonishment of defense counsel by the district court judge; the bizarre opening statement; the constant continuances and delays throughout the trial, which I am sure were held against the defense; and the belated presentation of important evidence. These harmful events resulted from Amador's conflict of interest and lack of preparation and now require reversal of this case... The evidence certainly indicated that Amador secured media rights while representing Rudin, which was a violation of the Nevada Rules of Professional Conduct.9...Amador was clearly more interested in obtaining information for his book and getting media attention than in developing Rudin's defense."

They also noted the testimony from Annie Jackson, Amador's assistant, and found new information there, as well. Jackson claimed that Amador did not turn over several of Rudin's files, containing diaries, witness statements, and pictures, to the public defender's office because he thought he might need the information in the future.

"I believe there is sufficient evidence in the record, without the necessity of post-trial proceedings, to establish that the defense was totally unprepared to try this case and that Amador had a substantial conflict of interest with his client. This was prejudicial to Rudin, and the result reached was unreliable."

Margaret appeals to the public in a letter she wrote from the Florence McClure Women's Correctional Center.

"The new trial I won [on] March 10, 2015, in the Ninth Circuit Court of Appeals has been blocked by the new NV Attorney General. Next week, their writ to the U.S. Supreme court will be filed."

She explains that, if her case lands in the 99% that skip review this session, it will return to the Ninth Circuit. Since they have already voted in her favor before, she hopes that once again, the NCCA will find her worthy of a new trial, and that this time their decision will be permanent. She maintains her innocence, and she continues to push for her appeal, and her opportunity to have her side of the story told.

CHRISTA PIKE

79

Christa Gail Pike, born 10 March 1976, currently sits on Tennessee's death row for the murder of Colleen Slemmer, 19, on 12 January 1995. The murder occurred when Pike was 18 years old. Pike and her then-boyfriend Tadaryl Shipp who was 17 at the time of the murder were convicted of Slemmer's murder and conspiracy to commit murder. Another friend of the defendants and the victim, Shadolla Peterson, also 18 at the time, was convicted as an accessory after the fact and given six years' probation after turning informant. Pike was sentenced to death by electrocution in 1996 and, at the time, she had the distinction of being the youngest woman ever to be sentenced to death, in any state and only the second women given the death penalty in Tennessee.

Early Life

Pike's life reads like a primer for depraved murderers. As a small child, Pike did not enjoy a healthy and supportive bond with her mother, Carissa Hansen, a licensed nurse, allegedly because of her premature birth. Whereas thousands of children are born prematurely and do not resort to criminal behavior Pike's birth was presented as evidence of one possible origin of her poor and troubled behavior. Pike's maternal grandmother was verbally abusive and Pike was raised by her alcoholic and abusive paternal grandmother until the latter's death in 1988 when Pike was 12; after which Pike attempted suicide by overdosing. She was then shuttled back and forth between her divorced parents' homes. In 1989, Pike was kicked out of her father's house for the second and final time due to her unruliness and the alleged sexual abuse of her father's then-two-year old daughter with his second wife.

Prior to the murder, experts assert that there were myriad indications that Pike was seriously disturbed; however, nobody who may have suspected this sought help for the increasingly disobedient and incorrigible young lady. According to Pike's mother, she was problematic since the age of eight and the two of them had a contentious relationship due to Pike's fluctuating and troubling behavior. Her mother asserted that by age nine Pike was growing marijuana in pots at their home and had been permitted to have a live-in boyfriend at age 14. At one point—in an effort to improve their relationship—Hansen suggested that she and Pike smoke marijuana together. Hansen mistakenly believed that cultivating a friendship with her daughter would cultivate the necessary bond Pike had been lacking her entire life. At one point, one of her mother's boyfriends whipped Pike with a belt which prompted her to wield a butcher knife against him before he was subsequently arrested. Hansen also admitted that Pike had repeatedly lied to and stolen from her. In several interviews with Hansen throughout Pike's trial and seemingly endless appeals, she admitted repeatedly that she was a terrible mother and should have spent more time with her daughter.

Pike's aunt, Carrie Ross, provided insight into Pike's upbringing when she testified that she disallowed her own children from associating with Pike because she lived in a filthy house that had zero ground rules and that Pike was a pathological liar of whom she was somewhat afraid. She also admitted that there was a history of substance abuse in Pike's family. Ross also stated that on the few occasions that Pike actually visited her she behaved like a little girl and engaged in Barbie and dress-up play with her eleven-year-old cousin. Further, there were some allegations that Pike may have been sexually abused but these were neither confirmed nor denied.

Pike's father, Glenn Pike testified that he did, in fact, kick his daughter out of his house multiple times; the last time being in 1989 after the aforementioned allegations that Pike sexually abused her two-year old half-sister. He admitted that he had signed adoption papers for Pike prior to her 18th birthday and that during the times she resided with him she was manipulative, disobedient, and dishonest.

After dropping out of high school, Pike began Job Corps classes in computer programming. Job Corps is a government-based organization that provides occupational and vocational training to underprivileged and troubled teens. It was at the now-defunct Job Corps center in Knoxville where she met Shipp, Slemmer, and Peterson. While Job Corps seeks to promote prosocial behavior and foster a strong desire among its participants to learn a vocation and secure a more promising future than might have been previously the case, this program is also known to cultivate criminal activity, likely due to the association among its participants; many of whom already had problematic behavior.

Evidence of Premeditation

On 11 January 1995, the day before the actual homicide, Pike told friend and co-Job Corps student Kim Iloilo that she was planning to kill Slemmer because she "just felt mean that day." Iloilo discounted Pike's statement as nothing more than merely talk; however, the following evening at approximately 8:00 p.m. Iloilo witnessed Pike, Shipp, Peterson, and Slemmer leaving the Job Corps center. When Iloilo saw Pike, Shipp, and Peterson returning at approximately 10:15 p.m. without Slemmer she, again, thought nothing of it. Even when Pike visited Iloilo's dorm room at 11:00 p.m. that night and confessed to killing Slemmer—as well as showing Iloilo what Pike identified as a piece of Slemmer's skull—Iloilo still failed to tell anyone. Later, at Pike's trial, Iloilo testified that while Pike was iterating the events of the murder she was oddly smiling, singing, and dancing around the room. The following morning Iloilo asked Pike what she was going to do with the piece of skull. Pike nonchalantly replied that she had it in her pocket and was, in fact, eating breakfast with it.

Pike also told another student, Stephanie Wilson, a similar account the following day and proudly described the brown spots on her shoes as blood. Not unlike Iloilo, Wilson failed to immediately report anything.

The Crime Scene

On 13 January, officers from the University of Tennessee and Knoxville Police Departments were dispatched to greenhouses on the University's agricultural campus in Tyson Park where a University grounds department employee reported finding, at approximately 8:05 a.m., what he assumed to be a dead animal. The gruesome discovery was a corpse that turned out to be Colleen Slemmer. She was naked from the waist up; her throat was cut; her head had been bludgeoned; and she had various cuts all over her arms, throat, and torso—including a pentagram that had been carved into her chest. Officer John Terry Johnson who testified at Pike's trial described Slemmer's body as so badly beaten that she was unrecognizable as a human being. He also stated that he thought he was looking at her face when, in reality,

Slemmer was lying face-down in the dirt and debris where Pike, Shipp, and Peterson had left her.

There was additional evidence and testimony that the crime scene encompassed an area that measured 100 feet long by 60 feet wide; an astounding 6,000 square feet in area. Despite the area being muddy and wet there was ample evidence of a physical struggle with trampled bushes, a considerable amount of blood, body drag marks, and hand and knee prints. Thirty feet from Slemmer's body was a large pool of blood which suggested that Slemmer was attacked in one area and then dragged to where her body was later found. Slemmer's shirt and bra were also discovered at the crime scene, as well as a bloody rag that Pike admitted to tying over Slemmer's mouth at one point to keep her from screaming.

Disturbingly, University of Tennessee police officer Harold James Underwood, Jr., who was the officer assigned to secure the crime scene, testified at trial that Pike and a few other females came to the scene between four and five p.m. the day of the discovery and before Pike was even considered to be a suspect. Underwood stated that Pike had asked why the wooded area was marked off, who the victim was, and whether police had any leads as to who the suspect or suspects were. He particularly recalled Pike's odd behavior—moving around a lot while giggling amusedly—and that she wore a necklace in the shape of a pentagram. The following day, during briefing when informed that the victim had a pentagram carved into her chest, Underwood reported Pike's behavior and necklace to his supervisors.

Autopsy and Findings

During Slemmer's autopsy, the medical examiner, Dr. Sandra Elkins, had to identify the victim's body from dental records because her head was so bludgeoned that she was unrecognizable. After cleaning up Slemmer's body which was clad only in jeans, socks, and shoes, and covered with dirt and twigs, Dr. Elkins began cataloging Slemmer's wounds. Due to the sheer number of wounds on her back, arms, abdomen, and chest, and the fact that following department policy which stated that each individual wound be assigned a letter of the alphabet, when Dr. Elkins reached double letters she, instead, individually catalogued only the most serious wounds and that there were innumerable other superficial and defensive wounds. Among the most serious cuts was a six-inch gaping wound across Slemmer's throat that was deep enough to penetrate the fat and muscles in her neck as well as the aforementioned pentagram. Additional injuries included fresh bruising which Dr. Elkins asserted was consistent with crawling.

Cause of death was ultimately attributed to blunt force trauma to the head. Dr. Elkins surmised that Slemmer's head was hit with the asphalt at least four times—two to the left side, one over the right eye, and one to the nose—which collectively resulted in multiple and extensive skull fractures. One of these blows was to the left side of Slemmer's head—which, according to Dr. Elkins, occurred with the right side of the victim's head against a firm surface. This blow only fractured her skull but also imbedded a portion of Slemmer's skull into her head and contained black particles from the piece of asphalt determined to be the murder weapon.

Even more tragic was Dr. Elkins' findings that none of Slemmer's other wounds would have rendered her unconscious and evidence of active blood flow around the wounds and blood in her sinus cavity indicated that Slemmer was alive during the severe torture she suffered before being killed.

Arrest and Confession

The police quickly connected Pike to the homicide thanks to the piece of Slemmer's skull discovered in Pike's jacket pocket. Pike had left this jacket hanging on the back of a chair in Job Corps Orientation Specialist Robert A. Pollock's office on 13 January after meeting with him about a misplaced ID card. Pike's jacket remained in Pollock's office from 4:00 p.m. on 13 January until 7:30 a.m. on 17 January. After learning over the weekend that Pike was a suspect in Slemmer's murder investigation, Pollock immediately gave the jacket to William Hudson, the Job Corps' safety and security captain who turned it over to Knoxville Police Department Officer Arthur Bohanan. At trial, Bohanan would testify that he found a small piece of bone in one of the pockets and presented it to Dr. Murray Marks, a University of Tennessee forensic anthropologist who was reconstructing Slemmer's decapitated skull and the piece in Pike's jacket pocket fit perfectly into an area where a portion of her skull was missing at the time of the victim's discovery.

When confronted with this evidence and subsequently arrested, Pike waived her *Miranda* protections and confessed to the murder and permitted officers to search her dorm room where the blood-soaked jeans she wore the previous night were found. Additionally, Pike led officers to a trash can at a nearby Texaco station on Cumberland Avenue where she had disposed of Slemmer's ID and a pair of gloves Pike had been wearing at the time of the homicide.

Pike's transcribed confession was 46 pages long.

In it, Pike admitted that there was animosity between Slemmer and her because Pike was convinced that Slemmer was a rival for the affections of her boyfriend, Shipp, and that Slemmer was trying to get Pike kicked out of the Job Corps program so she could have Shipp for herself. Pike also claimed that she had awakened one night to find Slemmer standing above her with a box cutter; however, there is no evidence of this allegation. Instead, Slemmer had repeatedly called her mother, May Martinez, to tell her she was afraid of Pike who she had awakened to find in her room and that she wanted to come home; to which Slemmer's mother said that she couldn't because she had signed a contract. Pike stated that she had only planned to fight Slemmer to stop her from running her mouth. On that fateful night of 12 January, Pike, Slemmer, Shipp, and Peterson signed the Job Corps logbook as they were leaving for an outing Slemmer believed was to smoke marijuana en route to a video store so that Pike and she could try to work out their problems.

When the group entered a tunnel at the edge of Tyson Park, Slemmer likely felt that something was not quite right and proceeded to ask Pike where they were going and whether there was, in fact, any marijuana. These questions irritated Pike who began the brutal assault shortly thereafter after they had gone deeply enough into the woods so that nobody could hear them that led to Slemmer's murder.

Pike confessed to initially slamming Slemmer's head into her knee and then throwing her to the ground where Pike continually punched, kicked, and slammed Slemmer's head into the concrete, screaming, "the bi*ch won't die" and that she wanted "to see [Slemmer's] brains flow." According to witnesses Shipp and Peterson, as Slemmer continued to plead with Pike to stop, Pike got angrier and more brutal. Slemmer offered to return to her Florida home, leave her belongings at the Job Corps center, and not tell anyone what happened; however, Pike became more enraged and yelled at Slemmer to be quiet because "it was harder to hurt someone who was talking to you."

In addition to the savage beating, Slemmer had been cut innumerable times with a box cutter and a mini meat cleaver (that Pike had allegedly borrowed from another Job Corps student) to her torso, arms, face, and back including having had her throat slit six times prior to the fatal blow that resulted from having her head crushed by a piece of asphalt. There was also a pentagram carved into Slemmer's chest; however, Pike asserted that Shipp had done that. Pike also confessed to "just watching Slemmer bleed" when the victim got up and tried to run away. Pike admitted to cutting Slemmer's back: "the big long cut."

After the murder, Pike stated that she and Shipp washed their hands and shoes in a nearby mud puddle to conceal the blood, dumped the box cutter, and Pike returned the meat cleaver to the person from which she borrowed it. This person has never been identified.

The physical evidence and co-defendant testimony suggested that the assault and murder lasted from 30 minutes to an hour and consisted of Slemmer repeatedly trying to get up and run away but was prevented from doing so by the co-defendants who also, as Pike testified, contributed to the physical assault by throwing rocks at Slemmer's head and holding her down so she couldn't run away. Later, Pike would testify that she heard voices in her head overriding Slemmer's continual screaming, telling her that she needed to prevent Slemmer from filing charges against her for attempted murder. Pike also admitted that at one point she thought she had heard a noise and went to investigate it to ensure that they were alone, as well as alleging that during the assault she heard Slemmer breathing in blood and jerking but did not let this assuage her anger as Pike continued her savagery.

Even more troublesome, a police video recorded after Pike's confession shows Pike smiling and providing extensive details about the crime at the crime scene, oftentimes mimicking her actions that evening. Many have said that her demeanor on the recording was eerily similar to that of a little girl who was excited and happy that she had experienced the best day of her life and had no problem talking about the events that transpired, the heinousness of her actions, and how she felt about it all.

The facts of the homicide are not nor have they ever been in dispute, thanks to an abundance of evidence. Pike's confession, and witness testimony at the trial.

Pre-Trial Examination

Prior to her trial, Pike was given a battery of assessment tests and examined by numerous psychiatrists including clinical psychologist Dr. Eric Engum who found her to be extremely bright as evidenced by an I.Q. of 111—in the 77th percentile of the general population—which he believed to be remarkable given her difficult childhood and lack of formal schooling beyond the ninth grade. Dr. Engum also found that

Pike had excellent reasoning, problem solving, language, and analytic skills, and was also quite adept at paying attention, sustaining concentration, and sequencing information. Dr. Engum concluded that Pike was legally sane and had no brain damage which has frequently been demonstrated to cause violent behavior in some individuals.

Of particular interest was that Pike was found to be marijuana- and inhalant-dependent and also diagnosed with borderline personality disorder. Whereas there are some similarities between borderline personality disorder and antisocial personality disorder such as impulsivity, irritability, aggression, and a self-image that fluctuates between self-aggrandizement and despair, there are several differences. Individuals with borderline personality disorder differ from those with antisocial behavior in that the former—which primarily affects females—is characterized by a lack of remorse, self-destructiveness, black-and-white thinking, alcohol and/or drug use or abuse, unstable relationships characterized by fear of abandonment and extreme swings between love and hate, difficulty in achieving academic and vocational goals, and are more likely to have been sexually abused; while the latter—which affects disproportionately more males—is characterized by a lack of affect and remorse, emptiness, and an ultimate goal of self-preservation.

Pike demonstrated all of the aforementioned characteristics of borderline personality disorder which makes it easier—but not justifiably so—to comprehend how her intense jealousy of Slemmer and fear of losing Shipp made her commit her atrocious acts. In addition to her fear of abandonment, Pike also abused drugs, was likely sexually abused, had contentious relationships, and displayed zero remorse. Dr. Engum surmised that Pike did not act with premeditation or deliberation in Slemmer's murder but, instead, in a manner that was consistent with borderline personality disorder. More simply, Pike had lost control. However, on cross-examination Dr. Engum admitted that Pike's deliberate luring of Slemmer, that she carved a pentagram in the victim's chest, that she brought weapons with her, and that she bashed Slemmer's head into the concrete does, in fact, constitute deliberateness.

That Pike was overjoyed and singing in Iloilo's room describing the murder while dancing around with the portion of Slemmer's skull Pike had taken as a trophy further supported Dr. Engum's diagnosis of borderline personality disorder because she had eliminated who she perceived was in competition for her boyfriend, Shipp, and, therefore, could continue her relationship with him. When questioned about the piece of skull Pike had taken, Dr. Engum said that Pike had no identity and her actions of taking and displaying the skull was a way to get recognition, no matter how misleading and distorted said recognition might be. In fact, after her conviction and sentencing Pike wrote a letter to Shipp which was intercepted by jail personnel that stated that even though she tried to be "nice" to Slemmer by bashing in her head instead of letting her bleed to death she was still sentenced to "fry."

The Trial

There was an abundance of evidence presented at the trial. Physical evidence consisted of crime scene photographs, autopsy reports, bloody clothing, and the piece of Slemmer's skull Pike had taken as a trophy. With respect to this skull piece, Dr. Elkins presented Slemmer's decapitated skull that was reconstructed by Dr. Marks to explain the victim's injuries. The skull presented at trial was complete except for a portion that was missing on the left side of Slemmer's skull. Dr. Elkins demonstrated that the piece of skull found in Pike's jacket fit perfectly into this spot, much to the chagrin of Slemmer's mother who, in a taped interview, stated that Pike was oftentimes giggling and passing notes to her mother and defense attorney during the trial, not unlike an immature middle-schooler.

At the trial, the State introduced photographs taken of Pike and Shipp at the Knoxville Police Department in which both were wearing pentagram necklaces similar to the shape carved into Slemmer's chest. It was presented that both Pike and Shipp dabbled in devil worshiping and other forms of the occult and that Slemmer was a sacrifice for the next day, Friday the 13th. Despite the presence of some type of satanic elements in Slemmer's murder, Dr. William Bernet, Vanderbilt University's psychiatric hospital medical director, testified that the evidence was that of "an adolescent dabbling in Satanism." He further concluded that the concept of collective aggression—or mob mentality—in which a group of people become stimulated and subsequently engage in some type of violent behavior was most assuredly at play in the events leading to Slemmer's death. However, Dr. Bernet ultimately stated that he did not have enough evidence to definitively surmise whether Pike had acted with premeditation or intent when she lured and murdered Slemmer.

Pike was ultimately convicted of first-degree murder and conspiracy to commit first-degree murder after a mere two-and-a-half hours of jury deliberation. The fact that the jury returned guilty verdicts for first-degree murder—and did it so quickly—demonstrate that jurors were convinced that Pike had the requisite mens rea, or mental capacity, to warrant a first-degree murder charge: premeditation and deliberation. Amidst the overwhelming evidence and utter lack of remorse for her actions Pike was sentenced to death by electrocution (Tennessee has since adopted lethal injection for executions but has the prerogative to utilize electrocution if the lethal injection drugs cannot be obtained). Shipp was sentenced to life without parole because his age at the time of the murder was too young to warrant capital punishment and Peterson turned informant and was given six years' probation for her testimony.

Pike's conviction was upheld by the Court of Criminal Appeals and the United States Supreme Court denied certiorari.

Post-Conviction

While incarcerated, Pike demonstrated more evidence of her depravity. In 2001 she tried to murder fellow inmate Patricia Jones by strangling her with a shoelace. Pike alleges that Jones repeatedly tortured her by calling her "fried chicken" and making various demeaning sounds as an affront to what Jones said was the sound that Pike would make when she was electrocuted. The final straw was when Jones physically threatened Pike's friend, fellow devil worshiper Natasha Cornet. Pike said that she jumped atop Jones and choked her with a shoelace so that the much larger and heavier Jones would get off of Cornet. By the time prison guards reached them, Jones was unconscious.

Pike was subsequently convicted of attempted murder despite her prior death sentence because any offense committed while an individual is incarcerated must be adjudicated. During this time, neurology specialist Dr. Jonathan Henry Pincus began investigating Pike's brain to glean some type of knowledge as to why Pike behaved and continued to act violently the way she did when she assaulted Jones. He asserted that every killer he has ever examined share three commonalities: brain damage, a history of abuse, and mental illness. Dr. Pincus alleged that Pike did, in fact, possess all three features and demonstrates all of the requisite features common to serial killers. There is much consensus among professionals that Pike would likely have been a serial killer had she not been caught the first time.

He also testified at Pike's attempted murder trial that her brain's frontal lobes are not "put together properly"; largely due, he claimed, to the fact that Pike's mother drank while she was pregnant with Pike despite denial of this by Pike's mother. It was also brought up that as a child Pike played at the slaughterhouse where her grandfather worked and that she was frequently subjected to pornography and horror movies on the home television screen. He asserted that all of these factors provide insight into how an 18-year old girl could act with such depravity as was the case when Pike murdered Slemmer.

However, the original trial judge, Mary Beth Leibowitz, stated that Pincus' "findings" of brain damage was curious as the defense expert at Pike's original trial who was trying to spare her the death penalty failed to find such evidence.

Forensic psychiatrist William Kenner testified that Pike had suffered from undiagnosed bipolar disorder, the symptoms of which were evident from the time Pike was a "sleepless, talkative adolescent" and likened her to an automobile with cruise control set at 120 miles per hour. Pike's post-conviction defense team alleged that this non-diagnosis justified her requesting a new trial.

In 2002 Pike sought to have her appeal legally stopped and to proceed with her execution. In June of that year Judge Leibowitz granted Pike's request and scheduled an execution date of 19 August 2002. However, a few days later Pike changed her mind and the Tennessee Court of Appeals subsequently stayed her execution. In October 2005, Pike's death sentence was affirmed; however, no execution date has been set at this time.

Pike was again in court in 2007 when her defense team headed by Donald E. Dawson asserted sought a new trial, alleging ineffective assistance of counsel in that her trial defense team failed to introduce evidence supporting Pike's alleged bipolar disorder. During this hearing, Shipp admitted to misinforming investigators and that he, in fact, was primarily responsible for Slemmer's murder. He stated that he was drunk and tired and just wanted the police to leave him alone when he put the onus of blame on Pike. Additional testimony from prior Job Corps student and the defendants' mutual friend Tyrone Comfort stated that Shipp controlled and abused Pike despite her assertions that he was the first male to protect her and she admired the respect and fear he elicited from others. Pike, however, was heavily medicated during this hearing for her alleged bipolar condition and the hearing was rescheduled for April 2008.

During her 2008 hearing, prosecutors portrayed Pike as a cold-blooded vicious killer who not only planned Slemmer's murder but prolonged it for sport, essentially playing cat-and-mouse with Slemmer by allowing her to get up and try to escape and then pushing her back on the ground for additional torture. Ultimately, her request for a new trial was denied.

Pike became newsworthy again in 2012 when she formulated an escape plan with the help of 34-year-old New Jersey resident Donald Kohut who frequently visited Pike in prison but the extent of their relationship remains unknown, and 23-year-old former prison guard Justin Heflin. In a joint investigation by the Tennessee Department of Corrections, the Tennessee Bureau of Investigation, and the New Jersey State Police after receiving information about the plan, both men were arrested and charged with bribery and conspiracy to commit escape, with Heflin charged with an additional facilitation to commit escape charge due to his job as a prison guard. Authorities discovered contraband evidence in the facility which could have only been brought in by a staff member and that Heflin was likely involved. Further investigation demonstrated that Heflin knew Kohut and that Heflin was receiving gifts and money for his assistance in the escape plan. Pike was also charged.

Even more recently, during yet another post-conviction relief hearing in 2015, testimony revealed that Pike was allegedly pregnant at the time of the murder. While this may be true it neither excuses her actions nor provides any potential evidence of legal insanity to justify an affirmative defense of not guilty by reason of mental disease or defect or guilty but mentally ill. Also during this hearing, Slemmer's mother requested the missing piece of her daughter's skull so she could bury the whole of her daughter but was denied as the skull piece remains a critical piece of evidence in Pike's ongoing legal appeals.

Since exhausting the state appeal process, Pike's new defense attorney, Assistant Federal Defender Stephen A. Ferrell, filed a

123-page petition on her behalf alleging that he constitutional rights were violated in both the original 1996 trial and penalty phase and that Tennessee's appellate courts ignored said violations. Among these claims is that capital punishment would amount to cruel and unusual punishment in violation of the Eighth Amendment of the United States Constitution because of Pike's youth, immaturity and mental illness. While Shipp—only 17 at the time of the murder—was too young to warrant imposition of a death sentence, Pike was not. Ferrell alleged that her trial lawyers were incompetent and failed to introduce evidence of mental illness, brain injury, and post-traumatic stress disorder. In response, the state Attorney General submitted a 90-page rebuttal repeatedly asserting that the state courts' ruling were all legally correct. As of the beginning of 2016, this battle continues.

Numerous video interviews of Pike over the past several years show her admitting that she was fully cognizant of her actions and that they were wrong. She stated that she felt as though she was taking out years of abuse on Slemmer and that she committed a horrible atrocity and deserves to be punished; however, she asserts that she deserves life without the possibility of parole for her actions; not the death penalty for the actions of three individuals. She has repeatedly stated that she wishes it was she who died and not Slemmer but such protestations are moot after the fact. One cannot help but wonder if Pike actually means what she says or is simply saying what she thinks others want to her. Knoxville Police Department detective Randy York who worked the case has said that in his lengthy career he has not encountered many people who he believes are evil but that Pike is, indeed, the personification of evil and that she should never be permitted to be around other human beings ever again.

Experts assert that the death penalty is not an effective general deterrent and debate over the morality and legality of capital punishment remains contentious and in the forefront of public discourse and debate. Currently, Tennessee is only one of 38 states which have the death penalty. Whereas women comprise 13% of those arrested for murder, only 2% are sentenced to death and, of those, only 3% are actually executed; primarily due to judges not wanting to sentence women to death. In Tennessee, only two individuals on death row have been executed—both males. The last time a woman was executed in the state was in 1837. Many currently believe that Pike will likely never be executed.

SHE MATES, SHE KILLS: THE TRUE STORY OF TAUSHA MORTON

97

ALISON YALE

AN AGGRESSIVE FLIRT

Dewayne Barrentine met Tausha Morton in early 2007.

She worked as a teacher's assistant at his son's daycare. A single parent, Barrentine would pick up his son and would be greeted by Tausha on a daily basis.

"Whenever I would pick him up," Barrentine said. "She would always make sure to step out into the hallway and give him a hug and say 'hey' to me. She made herself very noticeable."

Tausha gave Barrentine all of the hints that she was interested. The sideways glance, the smile that lingered just a little too long. But still, he needed extra coaxing.

"One of her co-workers actually approached me," Barrentine recalled when a woman in the hallway had passed him a note.

"She said, 'It's a phone number,' I said, 'To who?' She said 'Miss Tausha and she wants you go give her a call tonight. And it started from there."

Smitten by the forward nature of the sweet-faced single mother, Barrentine fell hard.

The two began dating and began living together within a month.

"She was really there for my son...," Barrentine recalled. "I had full custody of him. He would lay in the bed next to me ... and I would hear him say his prayers and he would pray for a mama." He would soon feel the same way about Tausha's daughter, Lexie.

"We weren't dating even a month and she said, 'Will you be my daddy?' And I said, 'Baby, I'll be whatever you want me to be...'"

From that moment, Barrentine became hooked as Tausha made him feel as if she really loved him. She did all the little things from kind words to love letters.

He soon began to realize, however, that Tausha had a manipulative, lying nature.

The tall tales began to pile up. She told Barrentine that she had a "Bachelor's degree in Criminal Justice" as well as an inheritance due to her from an inhertiance.

"It was from her granddad who was a federal judge who was blinded by a battery blowing up in his face. If he was a federal judge, surely his name would be on docs under Google somewhere, but I never found anything."

Barrentine grew increasingly suspicious with Tausha's stories. He did some online investigating and discovered that she had a previous marriage with a man named Mitch Kemp. He confronted her about it and she would state that she had been married five times before.

The two vaguely resembled each other, big Southern boys, "teddy bears" that were more than a little overweight.

After eight months of co-habitation, Barrentine caught Tausha cheating on him.

He promptly threw her out of his home.

"I called the Sheriff's department," Barrentine recalled. "I was like, 'look, I don't care what y'all do with her, she's got to get her shit and get outta my house.'"

Wanting retribution of some sort, Barrentine accessed Tausha's MySpace account as he knew her password.

"Dewayne gets on her Myspace account basically to mess with her," prosecutor Richard Hicks said.

After sifting through her e-mails, Barrentine would make a shocking discovery.

"I found two or three e-mails," Barrentine said. "And they were from Mitch Kemp's sister-in-law."

Mischele Kemp had written Tausha an e-mail with the subject "We're really concerned."

"How is Mitch doing? We haven't heard from you in over our year? We would like to hear from you. If we don't hear from you immediately we will contact law enforcement and media. It is not like Mitch to disappear

for years on end without contacting his mother and we have became extremely concerned. Please contact us. We are very worried about him and your entire family. Sincerely, MK."

Digging a little deeper, Barrentine looked into Tausha's "sent message" box and it did not appear that she had ever responded.

"Immediately, I changed the password on the account," Barrentine said. "To where she couldn't access it and I printed off all those e-mails."

His actions would prove to be something bigger than a missing persons case. He would bring all of this information to the local police chief in Florida who instructed him to keep things to himself as he sorted things out with the Boone County Sheriff's Department in Missouri.

WHO WAS TAUSHA MORTON?

Tausha Morton, AKA Tausha Fields, met Mitch Kemp in 2001 when she lived in Colombia, Missouri.

Mitch worked as a carpet installer and had been recently divorced after fourteen years of marriage.

"It wasn't long after he got divorced that he met Tausha," Mitch's brother Rick said. "I would say within months."

Despite their eleven year age difference, Kemp fell hard for the young and vivacious Tausha.

Tausha was the proverbial "people person." Most of her friends and neighbors described her as someone who would make you welcome and treat you as if you were a long lost friend.

"She was bubbly," said one of Tausha's former employers. "Friendly and inquisitive. She paid attention and asked lots of questions about you."

Tausha liked learning about other people. She, in turn, would be all too willing to share details of her own struggles.

"She told us how her whole family was killed in a car accident," Rick Kemp said.

Tausha had a way of getting people to feel sorry for her. She would come across as a heavily burdened individual who suffered a lot of tragedy. People listening to her story would feel compassion for her lot in life and do what they could to help her.

Mitch Kemp listened intently to Tausha's tales of woe, buying them hook, line and sinker. He wanted to help her. To be her rescuer, her knight in shining armor.

The two began to date and by September of 2002, Tausha gave birth to a baby girl.

Mitch loved kids and was ecstatic. He proposed marriage and Tausha accepted.

"They got married in Pensacola," Rick said. "It was a very easy wedding."

The marriage seemed to look okay from all observers. Mitch's family didn't have any misgivings about Tausha, her charm enabling her to get into their good graces, at least at first.

"She was a really sweet girl," Carole Kemp said, recalling her first meeting with Tausha.

But over time, his family began to notice a personality change in Mitch. Sister Mischelle stated that he wasn't "as playful as he used to be."

Family gatherings would "take a back seat to things that she wanted to do" according to Tracy Kemp, who blamed Tausha's ability to manipulate.

As work responsibilities increased for Mitch, things began to go south in their marriage very fast.

DOMESTIC LIFE AIN'T FOR ME

Bored that she was left alone with the baby, the high-strung Tausha needed an outlet.

She would arrive at her friend's gym, the Body Zone, with her baby in tow. Soon she began working part time at the fitness center.

It was there that she would meet Greg Morton.

Morton was more physically fit than Kemp but he fit the same profile psychologically. He had recently broken up with a longtime girlfriend and was be vulnerable to the manipulative charms of Tausha.

"Greg was despondent over his break-up," a family friend said. "But when he met Tausha, he kinda perked back up."

Tausha used the same seductive strategy on Morton as she used on Kemp. She detailed her tragic back story. She told him stories of being molested, of being raped.

She also told Morton in no uncertain terms that her marriage with Kemp was on the outs. Making herself look like the victim, she told Morton that Kemp had made her miserable. He was abusive, bothered her constantly and threatened physical harm.

"She told him a bunch of lies," one of Tausha's friends said. "She said she was getting him (Mitch) served, that they were getting divorced."

By February 2004, her allegations of physical abuse would be reported to the police department as Tausha filed assault charges against him.

"She said he abused her," Rick Kemp said. "By assaulting her, or slapping her or something."

Tausha informed police that she and Mitch had gotten into an argument. Then he hauled off and hit her.

Mitch Kemp would plead guilty to the charges and spend over a month in jail. Upon his release, he would be in for another surprise.

Tausha had moved out of the family home and moved in with Greg Morton, taking Lexie with her. Morton had own a farm outside of Colombia, Missouri, a sizable estate that he inherited from his step-father.

A custody battle then ensued between Tausha and Mitch for their daughter. The fight would get uglier by the day with daily phone calls between the two and their attorneys. She would refuse to allow Mitch to see Lexie and used the courts to prevent visitation.

But Mitch Kemp would not give up without a fight.

"If he had to go through the court system to do it, he would do it," Mitch's brother Rick said. "But that he was going to see his daughter."

Tausha would state that their divorce was finalized in August as the custody battle lingered on. She would then marry Greg Morton the same month.

But Morton had no idea what he was getting into and a "triangle" domestic dispute ensued.

Tausha had arranged to meet with Mitch in order to get some personal belongings. She drove in with Greg to the house of Mitch's friend where he was staying. Mitch confronted Tausha on the front porch where he immediately berated her, screaming insults.

Greg was waiting in the car at the time and went to intervene on Tausha's behalf. Mitch became further enraged and hit Greg over the head with a patio chair.

Retreating, Greg and Tausha sprinted back to the car.

Mitch, however, would disappear after that confrontation.

THE DISAPPEARANCE OF MITCH KEMP

It took awhile for Mitch's disappearance to hit home for his family members and friends. He was the type of man whom you would not hear from from awhile but would suddenly show up on the front porch.

He was dutiful about calling his mother Carole and when she didn't hear from him, she began to worry.

"We called the Boone County Sheriff's office," Rick Kemp said. "About two weeks afterward, probably. We told them that Mitch had disappeared."

The Sheriff's department did not think any foul play was involved. They offered assurance to the family that Mitch "probably didn't want to be found."

Boone County detectives came to that conclusion after they found out that Mitch was wanted for stealing some goods from a friend. They believed he disappeared in order to escape from repercussions of his actions.

Meanwhile, Greg and Tausha were living large. In late 2004, Greg put up his farm for sale which surprised both his friends and family. He treasured the land as it was bequeathed to him from his stepfather. Those close to him believed that Tausha had put him up to it.

In February of 2005, the sale of the farm finalized. With a $275,000 payout in hand, he and Tausha left Missouri, telling no one.

The Kemp family continued to believe that Mitch was not missing and that Tausha was involved somehow. They just didn't have any evidence or clues. Just a damn strong suspicion.

"Something had either happened to Mitch that had nothing to do with Tausha," Rick Kemp said. "Or something happened to Mitch and Tausha had something to do with it."

Both the Kemp family and Boone County law enforcement would then find locating Tausha and Greg to be a fruitless exercise. They literally disappeared from the face of the earth, wanting a new life. Leaving no trail behind, Tausha and Greg would move all the way to the Gulf Coast.

Greg, still smitten by Tausha, would get a tattoo of her name on his back as if he were a branded cow. With a new man firmly under her control, Tausha would go on a spending spree which included getting breast implants with Greg's money.

NO SIGN OF MITCH

By February of 2008, the Kemp family still had not heard from Mitch.

"They took a missing persons report," Rick Kemp said. "But the case went cold, quite frankly, because they didn't do anything about it."

But the Kemp family would not give up hope. They continued their search, turning to the Internet to look for any trace of their beloved son and brother.

They would search different social networking sites and court systems to look for any trace of Mitch.

They found nothing for years.

Until Mischelle Kemp found Tausha on MySpace, the social networking account.

"My sister-in-law found an account," Rick Kemp said. "That had Tausha's name and picture on it."

Mischelle immediately sent Tausha an e-mail.

"Tausha didn't respond," Rick Kemp said. "But Dewayne Berrentine did."

REVENGE SEEKING BOYFRIEND TO THE RESCUE

Dewayne Berrentine read through Tausha's e-mails on MySpace and began connecting the dots.

"Her little stories," Berrentine said. "Just because somebody lies to me, that doesn't mean I'm going to call you out on it immediately. I thought that she was coming up with these stories to impress me, maybe?"

Dewayne had discovered that Tausha had gotten around. He received some disturbing information from a man that Tausha had dated after she met Greg and before she met Dewayne.

His name was Keith Jones.

"I was in love with her and anything else didn't matter," Jones recalled. "You couldn't verify anything that she said," he says. "You know, and I mean there were a lot of stories."

Keith and Dewayne exchanged notes and stories about Tausha. They realized that she told them the same outlandish stories. But then Jones told Dewayne a story that he didn't hear before.

He described how Tausha revealed to him that she was involved in the murder of one of her exes.

"She had a few drinks in her," Jones recalled. "She said this guy had raped her and her daughter. And she apparently ... went to where he was and lured him back to her house ... and he walked in the front door. And that's when Greg shot him in the chest."

Both men thought the story was "so far-fetched" and because of the lies they always heard from her, thought nothing of it.

Dewayne did eventually confront Tausha about the allegation and she dismissed it out of hand, saying that her ex-boyfriend would say anything to throw a wrench into her new relationship.

Dewayne would change his mind about things when he opened Mischelle Kemp's e-mail message to Tausha, however. After notifying the authorities, he also wrote Mischelle Kemp back who in turn contacted the authorities in Boone County. The Sheriff's department then reopened the case. After doing some sniffing around, they discovered that Mitch had "fallen off the face of the earth" and had not filed taxes in over four years.

Finally, the Boone County Sheriff department realized that something was wrong.

INVESTIGATING TAUSHA

Detectives decided to start researching the background of Tausha.

They would discover that Tausha's parents were alive contrary to her account that they were both dead. Mitch's mother had spoken to Tausha's father shortly before her soon was to be married.

"She said, 'Mitch, we need to talk,'" recalled Rick Kemp. "You've heard a bunch of stories. Her family wasn't killed in a car wreck. They're alive. They don't want anything to do with Tausha. They say she's nothing but trouble."

Mitch dismissed the notion of his mother. He was totally smitten with Tausha.

Further investigations would reveal that Tausha had been married and divorced twice by the time she met Mitch Kemp. She would go onto have four marriages before she was thirty and the number of men she lived were numerous. Mitch had no idea that Tausha went from one man to the next man to the next. Even if he did, he was so smitten by her early in their relationship that he would have probably ignored the red flags.

Investigators would further discover that her divorce to Kemp was never finalized so she may have married Greg Morton while she was still married to Kemp.

Tracking her movements after she moved from Missouri proved difficult. Tausha and Greg were eventually tracked to Alabama.

The couple lived an indulgent lifestyle, buying luxury homes and cars on the $275,000 sale they profited after selling the farm.

But it didn't take long for them to blow through the money.

Needing more income to support Tausha, Greg would go to Mississippi in the hopes of finding clean-up work after Hurricane Katrina hit. After he left, Tausha saw it as an opportunity to cut him loose.

She had to find someone new.

"While he was gone doing Katrina," Barrentine said. "She was blowing through his money. Then he came home finding another man laying in his bed and he's broke."

Greg would immediately file for divorce.

MEN AND MORE MEN

Cut off from her money supply from Greg, Tausha would find work as an assistant at a day care center. It was there that she would meet Dewayne Barrentine.

She would follow the same modus operandi in her seduction of Barrentine, telling him the sob stories of her life. She described how Greg Morton would abuse her and how she escaped. She gave details on how Greg would try to "jump on her" and that they had "several physical altercations."

Agreeing to let her move in, Dewayne would meet Greg when he was helping Tausha get her belongings out of his house.

The two didn't fight. Instead, they spoke briefly and Greg would later tell Dewayne about how detectives from Missouri were looking to speak with Tausha.

Barrentine would eventually discover Tausha cheating on him and throw her out of his home. She would find a new boyfriend a few days later by the name of Denver Workman.

Workman left his job and his extended family from Florida to Wilmington, Delaware after Tausha begged him to do so. Then she wanted him to move back and Workman refused.

"She would yell, scream and throw things at me because I wasn't leaving," Workman recalled. "She would tell Lexie I was a bad person and to kick me. I bought her a bus ticket to Florida and let her borrow my truck that was still down there. She took the truck, and I never saw her again."

Police would finally catch up to Tausha in Dothan, Alabama and confront her about the disappearance of Mitch Kemp.

During her initial interrogation, Tausha would firmly deny having any contact with Mitch.

"What do you mean what happened to Mitch?" Tausha would ask detectives in bewilderment. "I haven't had any contact with him. None."

The investigators continued to press, however, and Tausha would try to insinuate Greg as having something to do with Mitch's disappearance.

"They had words on the phone," Tausha told detectives. "And then they had, they got in a fist fight one time."

After being threatened with the possibility of being put in jail and leaving her five year old daughter Lexie in the hands of the state, Tausha then placed the blame on Greg.

"Greg killed Mitch," Tausha said. "He told me."

She would then inform detectives that she wasn't there when it happened. She stated that Greg left about 45 minutes later after he had yet another phone conversation with Mitch.

Tausha would claim that she feared for both her and her child's life because of Greg's temper.

She would recall that Greg shot Mitch on the farm. Investigators played along, even paying for her plane ticket to fly from Alabama to Missouri in order to let them know where Greg had buried Mitch. But once she arrived, Tausha seemed confused by the layout of the farm. She could not pinpoint where exactly the body had been buried.

She was then released under her own recognizance back to Alabama while Sheriff deputies proceeded to dig up the farm to no avail. They used ground penetrating radar, cadaver sniffing dogs but came up empty.

WHERE WAS GREG MORTON?

While talks with Tausha revealed some clues, investigators were even more eager to speak with Greg Morton.

After ending his marriage with Tausha, he settled in St. Louis. He was going to school to become an electrician and had a new girlfriend.

He wanted nothing further to do with Tausha. When investigators approached him, Greg immediately invoked his right to an attorney and refused to speak further.

Detectives did not have enough evidence to charge him. But they had Tausha on the run and spoke to her again. This go around, they decided to employ a little psychological manipulation.

"But I tell you what," Detective Dave Wilson said while sitting across from Tausha in the interrogation room. "He (Greg Morton) automatically assumed that you talked to us. Now, we didn't confirm that."

"Why did he think that?" Tausha asked.

"Well, there's only...who knows?"

"But he said he thought he'd talk to you?"

"I'm going to ask you again. Can you take us directly to where that hole was?"

This go around, Tausha said yes. The Boone County Sheriff's department flew her in from Alabama yet again to Greg Morton's farm.

This time, Tausha led investigators straight to where the body was buried.

Mitch Kemp's remains were dug up and his identity was confirmed.

"It didn't surprise us," Rick Kemp said. "But we were all just blown away. I mean, I just didn't want to believe that my brother was gone."

Investigators discovered that Mitch had been shot numerous times and found numerous shell casings in the makeshift grave. They then went to St. Louis and arrested Greg Morton.

"He wasn't surprised when we showed up," Detective Wilson recalled.

Tausha was allowed to return home but investigators had a suspicion that she was more involved than she let on.

A VOW OF SILENCE

Greg strangely refused to rat out Tausha, remaining in prison until he was officially charged.

Tausha moved to Texas, however, and began dating someone new. Investigators would catch up with her again, however, and this time a heated ninety-minute interrogation would ensue.

Their probing questions would force Tausha to change her story about Mitch's murder completely.

"I did not do anything," Tausha said after detectives informed her that she would be charged with first-degree murder. "I helped you in every way I could possibly fucking help you.

"Tausha," Detective Wilson said slowly. "We got people who say, say otherwise, okay."

Tausha then changed her story again, stating that she was present when Greg murdered Mitch.

"I snuck around behind Greg's back and I saw Mitch, okay," Tausha said. "Greg had no idea."

She stated Greg would kill Mitch in a jealous rage after they returned from a hotel for a tryst. They then drove back to the farm and Greg assaulted Mitch before he got out of the car.

"He had a gun in his hands," Tausha said. "It was a black gun. Mitch started walking backwards. I ran inside the house and then I ran back outside. I saw that Mitch was walking backwards, and Greg was walking towards him. And Greg shot him. I didn't kill Mitch. I didn't want Mitch to die."

But the investigators didn't see it that way. They charged her with first-degree murder.

THE TRIAL

In June of 2009, Tausha had been imprisoned for over six months as she awaited trial.

Her bail was set at one million dollars.

Greg Morton then decided it was time to cut a deal. He broke his silence on what really happened the day of Mitch Kemp's murder. He would admit to his involvement in exchange for a more lenient sentence if he testified against Tausha.

In 2010, Tausha's trial began.

The prosecution's argument was that Tausha was the mastermind behind the murder, that even though Greg pulled the trigger it was Tausha that put the idea in his head. They also believed that Tausha's motive was to have sole custody of their daughter.

The defense would claim that Tausha was innocent and the victim. Her attorney was, in essence, using the same technique that Tausha used on all of her men. They would play on sympathy and hope that the jury would be as charmed by Tausha as all of her men.

GREG MORTON CONFESSES

Morton would take the stand and tell the jury exactly how Tausha manipulated him to kill Mitch.

"She's hysterical," Morton recalled. "She said Mitch raped her."

"What are you feeling, Greg, at this point?" Prosecutor Hicks asked.

"I wanted retribution. Tausha took charge and handed me a gun the net morning. She goes, 'I'm going to get Mitch, and when I get back, you shoot him.'"

"What were you going to do, Greg?"

"I was going to do what she asked me to do."

"They made a plan in that Tausha was going to go in town and pick Mitch up," Rick Kemp said. "And tell him that Greg was out of town."

Mitch arrived at the farm, thinking that it would only be the two of them. But then Greg emerged from the porch.

"I had a gun in my hand," Morton recalled. "I raised it and pointed it at him. I kinda paused I was kinda struggling with it a little bit. And then she started yelling at me to shoot him."

Greg believed that he was committing a protective act. He believed that Mitch was raping Tausha and molesting their six-year-old daughter.

"Then she said 'You got to get something to move him. Get something to move him with.' Greg recalled. "Then she said, 'Come on. You should have had this ready.'"

"And you saw that she was still struggling?"

"He was."

"So what did you do?"

"I shot him again."

"Was he struggling anymore?"

"It was over," Morton said. "I used farm equipment to pick up Mitch's body and we buried him in a pit. When we were rolling the dirty on Mitch she said 'Mitch Kemp is a piece of shit and nobody is going to look for him for a long time.'"

The defense would then call a neighbor who testified on Tausha's behalf, stating that she thought she was under Greg's control.

Greg then broke down on the stand and tearfully apologized to Mitch Kemp's family.

Over time, however, he began to realize that Tausha was a cunning liar. As he got to know her better, he realized that he had been duped.

"He'd been played like a fiddle by her," Rick Kemp said. "She did it to every man that she had."

Tausha was not called to the stand by the defense and the jury would find her guilty.

"I think she thought she was going to walk," Rick Kemp said. "She thought she could just get away with lying and manipulating people."

Tausha Morton was sentenced to life in prison without parole but is currently appealing her sentencing.